973.3
King, David C.
Benedict Arnold The Traitor Within

# Benedict Arnold

## THE TRAITOR WITHIN

David C. King

New Lights Press
P.O. Box 326
Hillsdale, NY 12529

Book and cover design by Jessika Hazelton

Printed in the United States of America

The Troy Book Makers • Troy, New York • thetroybookmakers.com

To order additional copies of this title,
contact your favorite local bookstore
or visit www.tbmbooks.com

ISBN: 978-1-61468-1182

To Sharon
For being the perfect partner

Acknowledgments

My thanks to Susan Novotny (Market Block Books, Troy, NY and The Book House, Albany, NY) and Eric Wilska (The Bookloft, Great Barrington, MA) for creating The Troy Book Makers and making so much possible for so many. At The Troy Book Makers, the advice and editorial work of Jessika Hazelton has been outstanding. And thanks to Jennifer Spanier for superb indexing.

I also want to acknowledge the help of the following in making this book happen: Sandy Flitterman-Lewis, Rutgers University, for ideas, assistance, and support; Lauren Losaw for assistance in locating resources; Karen Ball for research help; Nehoma Horwitt for encouragement, questions, and curiosity. And a very special thanks to my wife Sharon, *sine qua non*.

# Contents

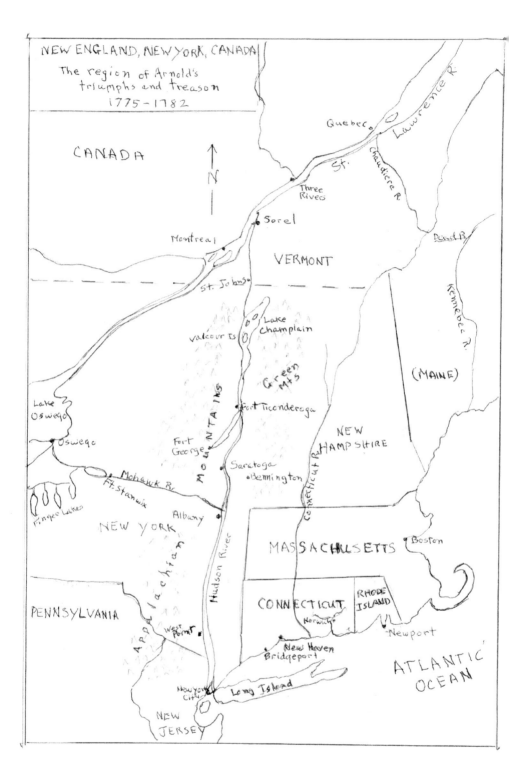

NEW ENGLAND, NEW YORK, CANADA

The region of Arnold's
triumphs and treason
1775 - 1782

CANADA

↑
N

Lawrence R.

Quebec

Chaudiere R.

St.

Three Rivers

Sorel

Montreal

Dead R.

VERMONT

St. Johns

Kennebec R.

Lake Champlain

Valcour Is.

(MAINE)

Green Mts.

Lake Oswego

Fort Ticonderoga

Oswego

Fort George

NEW HAMPSHIRE

Mohawk R.

Ft. Stanwix

Saratoga

Bennington

Connecticut R.

Finger Lakes

Albany

NEW YORK

Appalachian MOUNTAINS

Hudson River

MASSACHUSETTS

Boston

PENNSYLVANIA

CONNECTICUT

RHODE ISLAND

West Point

Norwich

Newport

New Haven
Bridgeport

ATLANTIC OCEAN

New York City

Long Island

NEW JERSEY

# Preface

Analysis cannot do justice to Arnold's story. It must be narrated
through its zigzag course during the four years before it took its
dark turn underground to treachery and catastrophe.

Carl Van Doren, *Secret History of the American
Revolution*. New York, NY, Viking Press, 1941,
p. 145.

From 1780, the year of Benedict Arnold's treason, to today, Arnold has
been viewed as the archetypal Dark Angel. Many of our wars have produced
traitors, but none has ever had such a powerful impact on his time or been so
vilified by history. Arnold, after all, nearly scuttled the American Revolution.
Only because of luck and poor timing did he fail in his attempt to turn over to
the British the complex of forts centered at West Point.

For four years, Benedict Arnold was America's most heroic and successful battlefield leader, hailed as Commander-in-Chief George Washington's
"fighting general." But as soon as his treasonous scheme was discovered, and
he managed to escape to British lines, Americans did all they could to diminish or forget his contributions to independence and to emphasize his guilt for
"treason black as Hell."

Over the next two hundred years, histories and biographies painted Arnold
as a tortured soul, whose need for money, along with a desire for revenge against
those who opposed him, drove him to treachery. Recent biographers have offered
kinder interpretations. The most prominent of revisionists has been James Kirby
Martin; his 1997 biography was titled *Benedict Arnold, Revolutionary Hero: An
American Warrior Reconsidered* (New York University Press, 1997).

Martin's major thesis is that Arnold had become convinced that the American Revolution was failing, largely because of bankrupt leadership; this failure

left the way open for America's new ally, France, to move in and take over if the British withdrew. He believed it would be better to restore relations with Great Britain rather than be ruled by the French. (The British had already offered home rule—and much of the Americans' demands short of independence.) Arnold even seemed to view himself as a sort of Pied Piper of turncoats who would draw thousands of discouraged rebels back to the fold. If this interpretation is valid, he emerges as a misguided Patriot, convinced he was acting for the good of the country.

Through the several interpretations of Arnold's life, there is still an air of mystery about the man. Even after reading all the explanations of his motives, one is left with the feeling that something is missing; the many different accounts are not satisfying.

My purpose in writing *Benedict Arnold: The Traitor Within* is to examine the mystery again, to find out what's been missing. This effort involves an examination of his life and military career to find what there was inside this proud, dedicated patriot that led to his apparently sudden decision to offer himself to the enemy he had fought against so valiantly for nearly five years.

The major discoveries I've made fall into three categories:

First, in reviewing the major events of his life, I've been struck by the patterns that emerge. Time after time, a great success was followed by devastating loss or defeat. Over time, he may have been so beaten down by defeats and by his enemies that he finally reacted with a wild desire to strike back.

Second, there were critical matters of timing. In terms of his desperate need for money, for example, this need is given as a major reason for his decision to sell out his country. The timing seems strange, however, because only a few weeks before his first contact with British headquarters, the government of New York State offered him, as a reward for his heroic services, a gift of two fine estates near Lake Champlain, plus 40,000 acres of land. With the likelihood of such a gift, did he really have to sell his services to the enemy for money?

Third, and most important, what was the actual role of his wife, Margaret "Peggy" Shippen? Most biographers (but not all) are certain that she was involved, but all agree that hers was only a supportive role. I'm convinced that she was deeply involved in the plot from the beginning; in fact, there is considerable evidence that she may have been the instigator or a co-conspirator. Much of my evidence is circumstantial, but the weight of that evidence makes the case.

Although I'm trying to add new clarity to Benedict Arnold's story, this in no way is designed to diminish his guilt in committing such a horrifying betrayal of all that American patriots were striving to achieve. In addition, I have only admiration for the contributions of modern historians and biographers who have combed through the vast historical record, a record that is maddeningly silent on several key questions. We have no documents to prove what was in his mind, or in Peggy's, as they wove their complex web of deceit and betrayal. But we do have enough evidence to peel away more layers of the mystery and to come closer to the truth.

# Chapter One

# Early Patterns

Few people in Colonial America began life with more advantages than did Benedict Arnold. By his mid-teens, however, young Benedict learned that advantages were not guarantees; fate could intervene in totally unexpected ways.

Born in 1741, Benedict must have learned early that his family held a special place in the society of Norwich, Connecticut. When the family entered church on Sundays, for example, he followed his parents walking with quiet dignity to the front row of pews, which was always reserved for them. For his father, the fourth Benedict Arnold, this recognition of status was gratifying because he had spent years striving to restore the family to a position of wealth and prestige following a period of declining fortunes.

In addition to belonging to one of the leading families in Norwich, one of the advantages in young Benedict Arnold's life was the promise of taking over his father's successful business. Another advantage was that the Arnold name was one of the most illustrious in the brief history of colonial New England. The first Arnold—William—had arrived in the 1630s, during the great Puritan migration to Massachusetts Bay Colony. Troubled by the strict rules of the Puritans, William soon joined the dissenter Roger Williams in his break-away move to Rhode Island. With his son, the first Benedict Arnold, William purchased huge tracts of land, then resold smaller parcels to the steady flow of new settlers. In addition to the family's growing wealth, Benedict I was chosen to succeed Roger Williams as governor of Rhode Island and served several terms until his death in 1678.

The Arnold fortune declined over the next forty years, largely because each head of the family (Benedict I, II, and III) divided their once-extensive land holdings equally among all the heirs. As a result, the death of Benedict III in

1719 left the prospects for the fourth Benedict limited to an apprenticeship as a cooper. The idea of spending his career making barrels did not appeal to Benedict IV, so he moved from Rhode Island to Norwich Town, Connecticut with his brother Oliver.

Norwich had become a booming port town, located upstream from the coast at the point where the Thames River divided into two. The town's location enabled it to compete with New London, on the coast. Norwich had better access to the inland farms and, by the 1700s, growing agricultural prosperity gave farm families the ability to trade for household furnishings and a few luxury items.

Benedict IV took advantage of the opportunities. He built a fortune as a merchant, purchasing ships to trade between the islands of the West Indies and ports in the American colonies. He also married a wealthy widow named Hannah Waterman King, and was enabled to take over management of the King mercantile holdings for his wife.

Hannah and Benedict IV seemed to have a warm and loving relationship. They had six children, the first, named Benedict, died within his first year, probably from diphtheria, also called "throat distemper." When another son was born on January 14, 1741, the parents followed a common practice by naming him the fifth Benedict, skipping over the deceased infant in the numbering. Of the six children, only Benedict V and a younger daughter, Hannah, lived to adulthood.

Benedict grew up in a close-knit and supportive family, which established patterns for a promising future. He received the best possible formal education, with the likelihood of going on to one of colonial America's few colleges, probably Yale, located in nearby New Haven. To prepare him for college, Benedict was sent away to boarding schools. In addition, his father's trade ventures—he was now known as Captain Arnold—offered a ready-made career for the boy.

### Mythical Boyhood

Practically all biographies of Benedict Arnold have repeated the many stories of Benedict's troublesome boyhood. One story, for example, related a favorite prank of stealing a baby bird from its nest, then torturing it in front of the adult birds. Another tale described Benedict tipping over a cannon on the village green, filling the barrel with gunpowder and lighting it. The resulting explosion nearly killed him and made the earth tremble. In another incident, he led a gang of boys in stealing barrels of tar, planning a great bonfire. When a constable stopped them, Benedict tore off his coat and challenged the man to fight him.

The many stories like these were designed to show that Arnold's boyhood revealed characteristics that would eventually lead to treason. It was not until the 1990s that the research of historian James Kirby Martin [James Kirby Martin. *Benedict Arnold: Revolutionary Hero.* (New York University Press, 1997)] showed that these tales first appeared in print or were mentioned soon after Arnold's treason was discovered, not before. There were no contemporary accounts of his antisocial behavior. Martin hypothesized that Revolutionary War veterans invented these stories to diminish Arnold's reputation as perhaps the greatest battlefield hero of the Revolution, and also to demonstrate that, even as a boy Benedict was aggressive, often violent, determined to have his way, and reckless.

An earlier biographer, Willard Wallace [*Traitorous Hero*, Harper & Brothers, 1954] suggests that some of the stories may have been true, "but were given undue importance by contemporaries eager to testify, after Arnold's treachery, to the blackness of his youth. He was in all probability neither better nor worse than other children, though perhaps more energetic, proud, and willful than most." 1.

## Upheaval

Although Benedict Arnold's boyhood may not have been as colorful as it is usually pictured, the pattern of privilege and promise is accurate. However, the youth's life did not remain smooth and predictable. A series of dramatic events led to upheaval in his personal life, destroying much of the hope for his future.

In the 1740s, much of New England was rocked by the religious upheaval that became known as The Great Awakening. Itinerant preachers touched off a period of highly emotional conversions to a search for God's grace. Benedict's parents became devoted to this strict observance of Calvinistic doctrine—avoiding God's punishment for sins. Hannah became particularly concerned with her son's moral state, constantly admonishing him to look after his soul.

Benedict did not accept much of Hannah's more Calvinistic new faith, but this did not lead to the kind of bickering and dissension that tore apart other families. Hannah made sure that Benedict went to good boarding schools; the second one was operated by her relative, the Reverend Cogswell. While she encouraged the schoolmaster not to 'spare the rod,' she was gentle in her religious instructions and reminder to her son. While he was away at the Reverend Cogswell's school, about twenty miles from Norwich, for example, she made sure he had plenty of spending money. In a letter in which she sent him thirty shillings (and the Captain added ten more, for a total translated into nearly 300 modern dollars), she admonished him that God would be watching to see how wisely he used it.

While the religious controversies of The Great Awakening helped shape Benedict's views on the role of religion in his life, far more shattering was the painful lesson that a family's social status did not protect them from the many epidemics that lowered life expectancy throughout Colonial America. Diseases such as smallpox, measles, scarlet fever, and diphtheria swept through entire regions, decimated populations, and left grieving families in their wake. The first of the Arnolds' children—Benedict—had died in his first year, probably of diphtheria, a disease that literally choked the victim to death. Hannah gave birth to five other children. There were two more boys: the Benedict who survived and Absalom King Arnold who died in 1750. Of the three girls, only Hannah survived to adulthood. The girls—Elizabeth, 3 and Mary, 8—died within months of each other during epidemics of the mid-1750s.

Hannah and Captain Arnold were devastated by the loss of four of their six children. They could take some comfort from the fact that Hannah pulled through the epidemic that took her sisters, and that Benedict was away at school. Hannah's letters to him gave the broad outlines of the events, but she told him not to come home, for fear that he too would become a victim.

The deaths of the two girls was particularly hard on Benedict's father. All four children had died before reaching age ten, and the tragedies had struck when his business was in serious trouble. The repeated warfare between the British and

French reached a new level of crisis with the Seven Years War (1756-1763). The family's business went into a steep decline from which it never recovered.

Benedict's father responded by starting to drink—not just in the manner of mid-18$^{th}$ century merchants, but to drink heavily, so heavily that within two years he was lost in a fog of alcoholism. Young Benedict, away at school, knew the situation was bad, but it was still a shock when he received a letter from his mother saying they no longer had money to pay for his school. The fifteen-year-old came home to his family and to the realization that his formal education had ended; there would be no advancement to Yale or any other college. The family's finances were in shambles, and it was soon clear that there would be no family business for him to take over.

Far worse for Benedict and his sister Hannah was the humiliation of seeing their father staggering through the streets of Norwich, the object of derision and jokes. On occasion he was arrested for public drunkenness and Benedict had to bring him home. The leaders of their church held meetings at which they chastised him and threatened him with excommunication. His wife Hannah, who had always held the family together, died in 1759 at age 52. That was the final blow. When Arnold's father died two years later, his passing was probably something of a blessing to his two remaining offspring.

The scars from those years remained with Arnold for the rest of his life. He hated the way people had behaved toward his father; and he developed a deep distrust of men in positions of privilege or power. Determined to restore the prestige of the family name, he became furious when anyone challenged his honor or his actions, sometimes "demanding satisfaction" through a duel. This wounded pride transformed him into a man driven by ambition.

## Apprentice Years

As soon as the family business began to fail, Benedict Arnold's mother Hannah had searched for other ways to give him a good start in a career. She persuaded two relatives—Joshua and Daniel Lathrop—to sign him on as an apprentice in their apothecary business. They were soon delighted with their young employee, providing him with steadily-increasing responsibilities and opportunities.

Apothecaries were more than pharmacists in the eighteenth century. The Lathrops, for example, sold surgical equipment and medicines to the British Navy and Army, but they also traded in an array of merchandise from fruits and fabrics to furniture and coffins.

Benedict's apprenticeship years have been the occasion for more tales about him in biographies of his life. According to the stories, he ran away from the Lathrops' apothecary shop on two occasions to join the New York Militia in order to fight alongside the British against the French in Canada. (New York paid higher enlistment bounties than did the New England colonies.) Although the fifteen-year-old boy never got into a battle, the biographers wrote, the episodes reflected several pre-treason traits: a desire to fight and to achieve military glory; a willingness to break the rules in order to achieve his goals; greed—enlisting in New York for a higher bounty.

Several recent biographers have stated that these stories are not supported by the historical evidence; in fact, they seem to be based on errors in interpreting the documents. The name B. Arnold appears several times in the enlistment rolls of the New York Militia, but there are different spellings of what could be thought as misspellings of Benedict, such as "Benedick" and "Bowdik." Physical descriptions don't match, none mentions the town of Norwich, and the occupation is listed as laborer and weaver. Benedict Arnold often said, "I was a coward until I was fifteen years of age." Biographer Jim Murphy has argued that "It's hardly likely that such a boy would dash headlong into a bloody fight."2.

More convincing arguments against his having been a runaway involve his relationship with his employers. Joshua and Daniel Lathrop were graduates of Yale and became highly successful in their business. They quickly saw that Benedict was intelligent, hard working and eager to learn. At first, he worked in the apothecary shop, where he learned the details of selling and dealing with customers. From the beginning, he lived in the elegant home of Daniel and Jerusha Lathrop. Mrs. Lathrop took to Benedict and was soon treating him like a son. She continued some of his schooling and instructed him in adult behavior, such as how to act toward people of inferior or superior position.

In terms of running away to join the militia, it does not seem likely that the Lathrops would tolerate having a runaway in their tightly run business or their embracing household. Also, they clearly had plans for Benedict. By the time he was eighteen, they were sending him on their trading ships to the West Indies and then to England. These experiences helped him to develop a knowledge of, and fondness for, ships and sailing. The Lathrops had such confidence in their apprentice that, when he was twenty, they helped set him up in his own apothecary business in New Haven, providing him with merchandise on credit valued at about $20,000 in early 21$^{st}$ century money.

There was one exception to the questionable reliability of the militia stories. In 1757 there was a general call to arms for all able-bodied men throughout Connecticut. The crisis, during the Seven Years War, occurred when a French army invaded from Canada; after capturing Fort William Henry, the French began pushing south toward Albany.

If young Arnold did get into a militia uniform and began marching, he did not get far. The French became concerned about their supply lines, withdrew to Canada, and the militia was disbanded.

## A Successful Young Man

In 1760, when Benedict moved to New Haven, he opened his small shop on the Lathrop model. He hung out a sign which announced:

B. Arnold Druggist

Book Seller, Etc.

*From London*

*Sibi Totique* ("For himself and for all.")

With the help of the Lathrops, he stocked his shelves with a wide array of merchandise—books, jewelry, cosmetics, and, as one broadside mentioned, "a very elegant assortment of mezzotint pictures, prints, maps, stationery and paper hangings for rooms."3. He also had an array of medicines and herbs, including "Spirits of Scurvy Grass," "James's Fever Powder," and "Francis's Female Elixer."

He had picked up some knowledge of healing practices from Daniel Lathrop and, by applying what he knew, he soon was being referred to as "Doctor" Arnold.

The business was successful from the start, and twice he had to move to larger shop spaces. His sister Hannah moved to New Haven, sharing his home and helping in the business. In spite of tales about Benedict chasing away suitors, Hannah remained dedicated to her older brother for life.

In his third year in business, Benedict formed a partnership with another rising young merchant named Adam Babcock. They purchased three good-sized ships and opened trade with the West Indies, Canada, London, and ports on the North American coast. With Hannah and a hired clerk to manage the shop, Benedict was free to spend much of his time at sea. A large portion of his profits came from buying horses, grain, lumber, and pork in Canada, products that brought high prices from the plantation owners in the West Indies. Molasses for making rum was one of the major products traded from the islands to New England.

The steady growth of Arnold's business was aided by the booming economy of New Haven. Between 1750 and 1765, the population quadrupled from 2,000 to 8,000.

Arnold loved the rough and sometimes dangerous life at sea. He was often away from New Haven for long periods of six months or more, and he relied on his sister Hannah to manage the business. The occasionally rough manners and language that "Captain" Arnold acquired led the established society of New Haven to consider him an "upstart" and "crude." Some, however, accepted him, including the Mansfield family; he married twenty-two-year-old Margaret "Peggy" Mansfield in 1767, and became close friends with her father. Margaret bore him three sons: Benedict VI, born February 14, 1768; Richard, August 22, 1769; and Henry, September 10, 1772.

The Arnolds seemed to have a loving relationship, although there were questions and some signs of trouble. While he was away on his long trading voyages he wrote romantic letters to her and agonized over why Peggy didn't write to him more often. He sometimes wrote impassioned exclamations, such as, "Oh, when shall we be so happy to meet and part no more."4. There are few remaining letters written by her and none indicating her reactions to the many stories of his mistresses or bouts of venereal disease, or tavern fights and occasional duels.

Over a period of thirteen years, from 1762 to early 1775, Arnold encountered countless obstacles to success. British taxes and customs collections nearly drove him out of business. He also had trouble collecting money owed him, and this led him to try to dodge creditors; these dodges almost cost him time in debtors prison.

Much of his trouble with British customs resulted from policies developed in the wake of Great Britain's stunning victory in the Seven Years' War (1756-1763). King George III and his ministers, in order to raise revenue to pay for the War and their expanded empire, launched a series of new acts, including the Currency Act, the Sugar Act, the Proclamation of 1763 (to prevent land-hungry settlers from moving beyond the crest of the Appalachians), and in 1765, a Quartering Act and the Stamp Act. For enforcement, the Royal Navy assigned ships and men to stop smuggling. In late 1765, Benedict joined other merchants in ignoring the Stamp Act and engaging in increasingly creative smuggling.

Arnold's business, as well as his marriage, suffered in the 1770s, when the story spread that the Captain was seriously ill with venereal disease. Although none of Peggy's letters on the subject survive, she must have been shocked by the lurid stories. Benedict not only denied the tales in his most ferocious manner, but he also persuaded several well-known business associates to sign statements supporting his protestations of innocence. The gossip soon faded.

Through it all, the business grew steadily and, by the time he was thirty years old, he was one of the wealthiest men in New Haven. He ordered the building of a handsome mansion and he was particularly proud of the structure's pillars which, he felt, symbolized his position as a leading citizen.

He also bought the Norwich house he had grown up in, which the family had been forced to sell during his father's business failure. Benedict had no use for the house, but it must have seemed a good way to demonstrate his growing economic power to the Norwichites who had been so unkind to his father. He then turned around and sold the house a year later for a substantial profit—a move that might have been his way of showing his disdain for the town and its people.

Arnold had made great strides in restoring the family's wealth, but he still had far to go in the matter of prestige or honor. He might have made gains by building political alliances with government figures who could provide support. His friendship with his father-in-law could have been a useful first step since Samuel Mansfield was high sheriff of New Haven County and could have provided introductions, but Arnold was not interested. This go-it-alone attitude turned out to be a serious mistake. His military career was to suffer frequently because he had no well known men in government to speak for him.

He did display a sort of political awareness in developing opposition to British Customs policy—an opposition joined by practically all colonial merchants. For these men, smuggling became a necessity in order for them to make a living. They did not consider smuggling to be a crime, but rather an act of patriotism; since they had no voice or vote in the creation of those taxes, the customs duties were not legal, so smuggling was not illegal.

The first sign of deep political conviction was in his response to the Boston Massacre in 1770. He was horrified by the shooting of five unarmed Bostonians by British soldiers, then further outraged when the soldiers were found not guilty. "Good God!" he wrote, "are the Americans all asleep and tamely giving up their liberties, or are they all turned philosophers that they don't take immediate vengeance on such miscreants."5.

Over the next five years, the dispute between Great Britain and her thirteen American colonies grew steadily worse. In December 1773, a band of Patriots took part in a widespread protest against British East India Company tea by dumping a shipment of it into Boston Harbor. The British responded swiftly. The port of Boston was ordered closed until the tea should be paid for. Thomas Gage arrived with 3,500 redcoats to enforce this and several other new laws, known as the Coercive Acts (or, in America, the Intolerable Acts).

Arnold became determined to be a major figure in any military action that developed. Perhaps gaining military prominence was a way to restore the honor of the family name. The first step was to form a militia unit in New Haven. His offer was approved and his men were delighted with their dashing new uniforms, designed by their commanding officer—Captain Arnold.

The early years of Benedict Arnold's story displayed a pattern that would be repeated throughout his life. Until his mid-teens, he seemed to be on a path that guaranteed success in life, including a formal education, which was rare in the 18th century, and a successful business that would be his. Then everything collapsed and quite suddenly the bright promise vanished, and he had to face the humiliation of sudden poverty, selling the family home, and witnessing his father becoming a shameful public spectacle.

As he would do throughout his future career, Arnold worked hard to overcome the obstacles. Within ten years of starting out, he had become one of the wealthiest men in New Haven, had built a magnificent house, and was happily married with three sons. Once again, his life was in a good place, with a promising future.

# CHAPTER TWO

# *Ticonderoga and Crown Point*

BENEDICT ARNOLD FORMED HIS NEW HAVEN MILITIA unit in 1774, calling it the Governor's Foot Guards. He outfitted them in striking uniforms of his own design, featuring scarlet jackets with silver buttons, white ruffled shirts, and black boots. Although the Guards were short of weapons and ammunition, Arnold hired a professional to train them in military routine. The idea of leading men into battle would be appealing to Arnold, and he thought that military glory would be a perfect way to restore the family's reputation.

In April, 1775, the people of New Haven were electrified by news of the fighting at Lexington and Concord—the opening battles of the American Revolution. Arnold's Foot Guards voted to join the militia units gathering outside Boston, but New Haven officials did not want to be involved until they knew more. Consequently, when Captain Arnold asked for keys to the town's magazine of military supplies, they refused. Arnold exploded. "None but Almighty God shall prevent my marching!" he shouted. 1. Within minutes he had the key and the Governor's Foot Guards were soon on the road to Cambridge, outside Boston.

The men were excited and confident. As Arnold proudly led his Guards through farm villages, and people emerged from their homes to cheer them on, he had a brief encounter with a Connecticut militia officer—Colonel Samuel Parsons—who was on his way home from Cambridge. It was a meeting that was destined to have a powerful influence on Arnold's dreams of military glory. Parsons told him about the many militia companies camped outside Boston with headquarters at Cambridge. But, he said, the patriots had little hope of forcing the British to evacuate Boston unless they could acquire artillery.

That need for artillery set off sparks in Arnold's mind. He excitedly told

Parsons about Fort Ticonderoga, a huge, star-shaped British fortress on the Hudson River that controlled the southern approach to Lake Champlain. The Hudson-Champlain corridor separated New England from New York and the West; it also formed the natural invasion route for any British force moving south from Canada. On trading trips to Montreal, Canadian merchants had told him that the fort had been badly damaged during the French and Indian War (1756-1763) and the British had done little in the way of repairs. There were now only a few dozen British soldiers guarding the crumbling battlements. Most important, Arnold told Parsons, the fort held nearly one hundred cannons, many of them made of brass. The story was much the same at Crown Point, a small fort built on a peninsula a few miles north on the lake.

When the two men parted, Arnold hurried on to Cambridge, his mind now filled with visions of military adventure. He was sure he could capture both Ticonderoga and Crown Point with only two- or three hundred men. Taking those forts would protect the colonies from British invasion and some of the cannons could be transported overland to the patriots outside Boston.

After finding housing for his Foot Guards, Arnold met with the Massachusetts Committee of Public Safety, the acting government of the colony. He described his plan for capturing Ticonderoga and Crown Point, and the committee immediately approved it. Arnold was made a colonel in the colony's militia and given written authority and money for raising up to 400 militiamen in western Massachusetts.

Arnold immediately set off on the 150-mile ride to western Massachusetts and eastern New York, with only a friend to accompany him. Other of his officers followed, planning to recruit troops as they went. "Colonel" Arnold was in high spirits, thrilled by the idea of leading his men into battle.

His buoyant mood did not last long. As he neared his destination, he was shocked to discover that another volunteer outfit was going to reach Ticonderoga ahead of him. Arnold himself had unwittingly set his rival force in motion: Connecticut's Colonel Parsons had reported his Cambridge-Road meeting with Arnold to members of the Connecticut Assembly. Without any real authority, these men appointed Captain Edward Mott to lead about sixty men to Ticonderoga; they also asked for a larger force to be raised by Ethan Allen, a big, tough frontier leader from the "Hampshire Grants" (soon to be renamed Vermont).

Riding like a man possessed—and nearly killing his horse—Arnold caught up with Allen and his men on May 8. Ethan Allen's followers were known as the "Green Mountain Boys"—a rowdy, often unruly bunch, but willing to follow Allen anywhere. Allen was one of the most colorful figures of the Revolution. He stood well over six feet tall, had immense strength, and possessed a great capacity for alcohol, especially his favorite drink, called a "Stonewall" (rum mixed with hard cider). He was not a smart man, but he was clever, especially at advancing his own reputation.

When the two leaders finally met, Arnold expressed his fury and claimed to have the only legitimate authority to lead. But Allen had nearly 200 men around him, while Benedict Arnold was still waiting for his first recruits to arrive. After hours of heated argument, Allen shrewdly offered co-leadership to his rival, because he recognized that Arnold's written orders from Massachusetts were the only legitimate authority. Arnold was far from pleased, but he knew he had no choice but to agree. Allen's Green Mountain Boys, who had little regard for Colonel Arnold, were ready to mutiny until Allen persuaded them to accept the compromise.

The attack on Fort Ticonderoga turned into something of a comedy. On the night of May 9-10, 1775, the co-leaders managed to get about eighty men across Lake Champlain in rowboat relays by the time dawn approached. Imagine the shock of the lone British sentry when he confronted Arnold in his bright scarlet coat and big Ethan Allen decked out in yellow breeches and a striking green coat with over-sized gold epaulets.

The sentry quickly retreated and Green Mountain Boys poured through the gate. Allen and Arnold encountered the sleepy second-in-command as he struggled to pull on his pants. When he asked by what authority the two men demanded surrender of the fort, Allen bellowed, "In the name of the great Jehovah and the Continental Congress!" When they found the fort commander, he quickly saw that his position was hopeless and surrendered the fort.

The attack had lasted about ten minutes. There were no casualties. Allen sent a small force under towering Seth Warner north to Crown Point, which also quickly surrendered.

The next few days were hard for Benedict Arnold. Most of the Green Mountain Boys were interested only in looting, and when he tried to stop them, they threatened to shoot him. In a report to the Massachusetts Committee of Public Safety, Arnold wrote: "There is here at present near one hundred men, who are in the greatest confusion and anarchy, destroying and plundering private property, committing every enormity, and paying no attention to the publick service ..." 2.

The whole affair was a bitter disappointment for Arnold. His vision of leading his men in an assault on an enemy fort had turned into a mockery. He thought of simply leaving and going home, but he decided to hang on, and by the middle of May, events finally began to go his way. Once the Green Mountain Boys had gathered as much plunder as they could, they began drifting eastward toward their homes. At the same time, Arnold's recruits began to arrive and soon outnumbered Allen's men, enabling Arnold to restore a measure of military discipline.

As his confidence returned, Arnold decided to launch a new offensive. Lake Champlain was still controlled by the British and they could always use the lake, plus the Hudson River, to launch an invasion into the heart of America, separating New England from New York and the rest of the colonies. The British controlled the lake largely because they had a 70-ton warship based at St. Johns, about 25 miles north of the Canadian border.

Arnold's plan, the first of several daring adventures that would soon make him famous, was to make his way north, raid St. Johns, and seize the British ship. The plan was made possible when a good-sized schooner sailed up to Ticonderoga's dock, with Arnold's friend—and one of his captains—Eleazer Oswald—at the helm. Some of Allen's Green Mountain Boys had captured the schooner, but they knew nothing about sailing it, so they turned it over to Oswald.

On May 14, Arnold was sailing north on the schooner, which he renamed the *Liberty*. Although the schooner was small it felt quite natural to him to be at the helm of a ship again. He had armed *Liberty* with six swivel guns and four small carriage guns; he also had two *bateaux*—small open boats that were rowed or, in shallow water, poled.

The *Liberty* reached the Canadian border on the night of May 17, but lack of wind prevented the schooner from going further. Overnight, Arnold chose thirty-five men to row the two bateaux down the Richelieux River to St. Johns. At dawn, they charged into the fort, where they found only a dozen unsuspecting redcoats. Arnold made them prisoners and then led his men onto the 70-ton war sloop and easily overwhelmed the crew.

Hearing from their prisoners that British troops were coming from Montreal, Arnold and his men quickly set sail, and in a short time reached the safety of Lake Champlain. In addition to the ship, which Arnold renamed the *Enterprise*, they had captured five more *bateaux* and a few more brass cannons.

Arnold's bold raid into Canada had been carried out with remarkable speed and efficiency. Unlike the mob at Ticonderoga, his men were disciplined and avoided pillaging. His success assured that the British could not launch an invasion down the Champlain-Hudson corridor until they could construct ships on Lake Champlain. Only later, after the Battle of Saratoga in 1777, would it become clear that Benedict Arnold's efforts to control Champlain helped the patriots gain valuable time.

The attacks on Ticonderoga, Crown Point, and St. Johns had yielded nearly 200 cannons. As soon as he was back at Ticonderoga, Arnold had crews start work on building wheel carriages for transporting the best 57 cannons south to Albany. From there, the artillery would be painfully dragged across Massachusetts to the Boston area. The following spring, the commander-in-chief—George Washington—positioned the cannons on the heights overlooking Boston. This display of power was enough to persuade the British to evacuate Boston and sail north to the safety of Nova Scotia (Canada).

## Arnold's Hard Lessons in Politics

Arnold did not have long to enjoy his brilliant military feat. First, the British were outraged by the three audacious attacks on British property at Ticonderoga and Crown Point, as well as an invasion of Canada. In London, British leaders said that the attacks succeeded only because British defenders were totally unprepared since they had no reason to expect attacks that were really acts of war. They denounced Benedict Arnold as a "horse jockey"—a man who did nothing more than buy and sell horses. They also had little respect for a man of low social standing; and they were certain that Arnold and his followers would break and run when they confronted British troops.

The attacks also upset many Americans, including members of the new Continental Congress, which began meeting in Philadelphia on the very day that Allen and Arnold captured Fort Ticonderoga. Many of the delegates had felt justified in taking up arms to defend their rights, as they had done at Lexington and Concord. They were planning on resolving their differences with King George III and Parliament. The brash action of Arnold, Allen and the others would make a peaceful settlement more difficult, if not impossible.

If Arnold was stunned by these reactions to his military achievements, they were nothing compared to the abuse he encountered in the weeks that followed. Although he was skilled as a soldier and as a ship's captain, as well as a very successful merchant, he was a political novice. He had no political allies in Connecticut or Massachusetts; no one in government or the military was ready to speak up for him. On the contrary, there were several men who were determined to destroy him politically. He turned out to be an easy target.

Ethan Allen displayed his shrewdness in his reports about the capture of Ticonderoga. His written account to New York's government stated, "I took the fortress of Ticonderoga," but to give the event legitimacy, he added, "Colonel Arnold entered the fortress with me." 3. But in his report to the Massachusetts Provincial Congress, he did not mention Arnold at all, although he did find ways to praise his allies. James Easton, for example, "behaved with great zeal and fortitude . . . in the assault"; John Brown " .

BENEDICT ARNOLD: THE TRAITOR WITHIN

. . was an able counselor, and was personally in the attack"; and the Green Mountain Boys "behaved with resistless fury." 4.

Allen was also clever in having these reports delivered by hand, with Easton going to the Massachusetts Congress. (Easton had asked Arnold to promote him to colonel, but Arnold thought him a coward and so turned him down.) From Ethan Allen's perspective, Easton was the perfect person to talk about Benedict Arnold. While Arnold was preparing to attack St. Johns, Easton was appearing before the Massachusetts Provincial Congress elaborating on his written report about Ticonderoga and completing his character assassination of Arnold.

Allen had been careful not to criticize Arnold. That task was taken care of by Edward Mott, who had led the Connecticut militiamen to Ticonderoga. In his report, Mott said that Arnold's attempts to assume command of the attacking force had nearly caused a mutiny among the men. Only the leadership of Allen and Easton had saved the mission from the near-disaster caused by Benedict Arnold.

Weeks of debate and confusion followed—in Congress and also in the governments of Massachusetts and Connecticut. Some members of government wanted reconciliation with England, which would probably involve returning Forts Ticonderoga and Crown Point to the British. Other delegates believed that the British would soon launch a major invasion from Canada south down the Champlain-Hudson River corridor; they believed it was best to attack first.

Through these weeks from May to July, Benedict Arnold's reputation continued to take a beating from the attacks by Allen, Easton, Mott, and Brown. In late June, the beleaguered and disgusted Arnold resigned his commission. Easton was promoted to colonel and given command of Arnold's regiment, John Brown was made a major in the same regiment, and Ethan Allen was hailed as the "Hero of Ticonderoga." Their victory over Arnold could not have been more complete.

The bloodless victory at Ticonderoga and Crown Point was a momentous one, but it revealed one of the patterns of Benedict Arnold's life. He hoped to emerge as the leader of the victory, but after the hatchet job on his character by Allen, Easton, and others, it was Ethan Allen who became known as the hero.

Out of the political chaos of that spring, surprising new thinking emerged: Congress decided to launch an invasion of Canada. The hope was that the new Continental Army, commanded by General George Washington, could conquer Canada, perhaps making it the fourteenth colony, before large numbers of British troops arrived. Leaders of Congress did not mention Benedict Arnold as possible leader of the invasion force. Instead, they selected Major General Philip Schuyler of New York, who had served in Congress and in the French and Indian War.

Arnold was deeply disappointed at being passed over, but he decided to meet with Schuyler in the hope that the aristocratic New Yorker might offer him something. Schuyler already had a good opinion of him, having learned about his daring raid on St. Johns. The two men met at Schuyler's sprawling estate near Albany and the major general was pleased by Arnold's detailed knowledge of the Champlain region. Arnold, in turn, could hope that Schuyler might help him obtain a new commission.

Just as Schuyler's friendship seemed to offer Arnold a bit of hope, he was hit with a devastating personal tragedy: news reached him at Schuyler's estate that his wife Peggy had died suddenly on June 19—two weeks earlier. Three days later, her father, "Papa" Mansfield, who had become Arnold's close friend, also died. Peggy, who was only thirty, probably succumbed to one of the epidemic fevers that frequently swept through the colonies.

Arnold was overwhelmed with grief. He had always looked forward to being with her in their magnificent New Haven home, "where mutual love and friendship doubled our joys . . ." 5. He left Albany for the lonely ride home, eager to see his sister Hannah and his three young sons (the oldest was just seven). He was relieved to find that Hannah had taken care of the funeral arrangements and had kept his business affairs in good order.

For the next few weeks, Arnold was in despair. His life had reached its lowest point. His courageous efforts in the patriot cause had ended in defeat and humiliation, and the loss of his beloved wife left an aching hole in his life. But

Hannah refused to let him give up. She told him that she would do her best to be a "good mother" to the boys and would maintain his home as well as his various business interests.

Arnold's natural resilience took over, and by late July he was ready for action. Once again, he headed for Cambridge, with a new plan already taking shape in his mind: The planned invasion of Canada, to be led by General Schuyler, would use the Hudson-Champlain corridor; Arnold planned to meet with General Washington and propose leading a second invasion of Canada, this one through the forests of Maine. It was a bold scheme—and that made it typical of Benedict Arnold.

# CHAPTER THREE

## The Wilderness March

At Cambridge, General Washington readily approved Arnold's plan to lead a second invasion of Canada. They agreed on a force of 1,100 men that would march through the Maine wilderness, following the Kennebec River and other waterways to the Chaudiere River, which would lead straight to Quebec, the capital of British Canada.

The main American army, under General Schuyler, would advance from the west, through St. Johns and Montreal, then meet up with Arnold's force outside Quebec.

While Benedict had been excited about the Ticonderoga campaign, at least until events and men turned against him, he considered this invasion of Quebec "the opportunity of a lifetime." He would plan it and lead it, responsible only to General Washington, not to political figures.

This "march" through the Maine wilderness was destined to become one of the great survival stories in America's history. It would also make Benedict Arnold a national hero.

As soon as Washington and Schuyler approved the plan, Arnold worked with ferocious speed to prepare for the journey. Timing was important. The Schuyler-led troops were already in Canadian territory. It was necessary for both armies to reach Quebec at nearly the same time in order to have a coordinated attack.

While waiting for Schuyler's approval, Arnold had carefully selected regiments and individuals from the thousands of men camped around Cambridge, keeping the British hemmed in around Boston. The heat of late summer, the boredom of the siege, and the promise of action, brought far more volunteers than were needed.

Arnold selected three companies of riflemen and ten companies of muskets. While most troops in the American Revolution used muskets, the riflemen formed a distinctive breed and soon acquired a romantic image as well as a reputation as expert marksmen. Their long rifles had gun barrels with interior grooves—or "rifles"—which caused the bullet to spin and to leave the gun in a straight line. Muskets had smooth barrels which allowed the bullet to rattle from side to side, causing the shell to leave the barrel in an erratic flight.

The difference in the weapons was important. At long range, the rifles were remarkably accurate. British troops soon called them "the world's deadliest widow-makers." Rifles, however, were less effective in close combat, partly because they took more time to load. Muskets, on the other hand, were useful at short range where the lack of accuracy was less noticeable; muskets could also be fitted with bayonets, while rifles could not.

Arnold's three companies of riflemen, two from Pennsylvania and one from Virginia, were rough outdoorsmen. They wore fringed hunting shirts, Indian leggings, broad-brimmed hats, and moccasins, with scalping knives and tomahawks strapped to their belts. As snipers, and for launching an attack, riflemen had no equals. The riflemen were met with some derision because of their clothing when they had first arrived at Cambridge, but they quickly earned respect. Arnold placed Captain Daniel Morgan in command of all the rifle companies. Morgan was a big, barrel-chested frontiersman, with a booming voice and a commanding presence. He was to become one of the outstanding generals of the Continental Army.

By mid-September, Arnold had his army ready to go. He had worked tirelessly to overcome countless difficulties in getting to this point, including arranging money for many of the men who were worried because they would have no pay due them until they were in Canada. He had all the men, except the rifle companies, supplied with new coats, linen frocks, blankets, shoes, guns, and tents.

On the crisp, sun-filled morning of September 19, 1775, there was a sense of excitement in the air as crowds gathered to watch 1,050 troops board the eleven fishing boats that would carry them up the coast to the Kennebec River. A surprising number of men kept journals, including Private Abner Stocking, who described the departure: "We got underway with a pleasant breeze, our drums beating, fifes playing, and colours flying. Many pretty girls stood upon the shore, I suppose weeping for the departure of their sweethearts. At eleven o' clock . . . we left the entrance of the harbor and bore away for the Kennebec River." 1.

The sea journey was hampered by thunderstorms, dense fogs, a difficult entry to the Kennebec, plus seasickness. After three days, the boats anchored at Reuben Colburn's shipyard. Early in September, Arnold had met with Colburn in Cambridge and ordered the building of 200 *bateaux*. These were simple boats that could be propelled by oars, paddles, or poles. Each bateau was large enough to carry six or seven men, plus supplies.

All 200 boats were completed, but when Arnold saw how poorly they were made, he flew into a rage. In the rush to finish their task, the builders had used green lumber that quickly warped, the boards pulled apart, and leaks developed. Although Colburn's men, with help from carpenters in Arnold's force, made what repairs they could, and added twelve new boats, it was clear that the bateaux were going to be a constant problem. That was only the first of countless disasters that were soon to threaten the lives of the entire expedition.

After transferring the supplies from the fishing boats to the bateaux, they were ready for what Arnold called "our plunge into the wilderness." He had divided the army into four companies. Two advance companies set out on September 28th, the rest following a day later. Arnold traveled by canoe so he could move back and forth along the long line of march.

When they reached one of the last clusters of settlers' cabins, the inhabitants helped him understand the second devastating problem: In mapping out the expedition, Benedict had relied on the only known charts, which had been made in 1761 by a British engineer, Lieutenant John Montresor. His calculation of the distances turned out to be far off. He had estimated the total distance to Quebec to be 180 miles; the actual distance would turn out to be 385 miles—more than double the estimate.

Benedict did not seem troubled by the new estimate of the distance. He had tremendous confidence in his ability to overcome obstacles. In physical terms, he was very strong and athletic. (Although many accounts describe him as short and stocky, about 5'4" in height, that height was at least average, and some descriptions place him at 5'7" or even 5'9"—well above average. His broad shoulders may have made him appear stocky.) From boyhood, he had always astounded people with his abilities in running, swimming, jumping, climbing, or riding.

Arnold also was completely fearless. He seemed to have a deep-seated faith in his destiny or fortune. Particularly in his military life, he felt that as long as he could act decisively, he would succeed. In terms of the journey ahead, he boldly told his men: "I believe, by the best information I can procure, we shall be able to complete the march in twenty days." 2.

The men, however, soon began to encounter the first of the incredible obstacles that were to threaten the march. Daily travel, without special problems, was grueling. Caleb Haskell, another diarist, wrote early in the march: "We begin to see that we shall have a scene of trouble to go through in this river, the water is so swift and the shoal full of rocks, ripples and falls, which oblige us to wade a great part of the way." 3.

The very first of the many waterfalls they were to encounter—Ticonic Falls—revealed more severe hardships: the portages. The bateaux were hauled out of the river, and nearly 65 tons of supplies were taken out. Handspikes were passed beneath each 400-pound boat, fore and aft, and four men struggled to carry the clumsy craft to a point above the falls.

At the next portage, on October 1st, the men were up to their waists in the frigid, swirling water. Their hands, constantly wet, became blistered and raw from hauling the bateaux. When they finally lay down to sleep that night, they were still soaked through; they awoke to find their clothes frozen, one wrote, "as thick as a pane of glass."

After more difficult portages, Benedict realized the men were exhausted by how hard he was pushing them. He constantly had in mind the solemn warning from Washington as Arnold prepared to leave: "The safety and welfare of the whole continent might depend upon the success of the Kennebec expedition." 4.

BENEDICT ARNOLD: THE TRAITOR WITHIN

The men were relieved when Arnold called for a halt of a few days to repair the bateaux and examine the food supplies. The boats had been badly battered by rocks and rough water, often causing the seams to split. Dr. Isaac Senter, a 22-year-old surgeon from New Hampshire, another diarist, described the results:

> ... By this time, many of our bateaux were nothing but wrecks, some stove to pieces, etc. The carpenters were employed repairing them, while the rest of the army were busy in carrying over the provisions, etc. ... The [dried] fish lying loose in the bateaux ... were spoiled by being continually washed with fresh water running into the bateaux. The bread casks not being waterproof, admitted the water in plenty, swelled the bread, bursts the casks, as well as soured the whole bread. 5.

Dr. Senter and Arnold also discovered that the salt beef had been poorly prepared by the packers and nearly all of it had to be thrown away.

After repacking the remaining provisions, the army pushed on. They were soon battered by weather and the wilderness more severely than ever. On October 11th, the three lead divisions began struggling through the Great Carrying Place, where they left the Kennebec River. Heavy rains turned the land into a quagmire. The men had to push west across three ponds separated by long, hard portages. The men carried bateaux and supplies on their backs over flinty rock ledges and into lowland marshes where they were often hip deep in mud and water. Many men were becoming ill with nausea and diarrhea, some from drinking brackish marsh water, others from spoiled provisions.

The tireless Benedict Arnold seemed to be everywhere as the men struggled over the rugged terrain, helping a group laboring uphill with a bateau, lifting a trooper who slipped into a deep swamp, aiding another with a twisted knee who could no longer walk. Wherever he went, he encouraged the men with kind and cheerful words, exhibiting his extraordinary strength and determination.

After the Great Carrying Place, they reached the Dead River, which brought more and different hardships. The river was constantly winding and, following three days of torrential rain, flooded its banks more than a mile on either side. The men who were marching by land had to make huge detours, while on the raging river several bateaux were swamped and their supplies lost.

In a matter of a few days the expedition had reached the breaking point. The men were soaked, and the weather turned bitterly cold, with several inches of snow replacing the rain. They were so short of food that, on some days, the men had nothing to eat but what they called "bleary"—nothing but flour and water, without salt.

Young Dr. Senter, near the 1$^{st}$ of November, wrote in his diary about what he called "almost the zenith of distress":

> Several had been entirely destitute of either meat or bread for many days. . . . Almost anything was rendered admissible. . . . In the company was a poor dog who had lived through all the tribulations [and now] became a prey for the sustenance of the assassinators. This poor animal was instantly devoured, without leaving any vestige of sacrifice. Nor did the shaving soaps, pomatum, and even lip salve, leather of their shoes, cartridge boxes, etc. share any better fate . . . 6.

In pouring rain, Arnold met with the officers nearest to him, huddled around a feeble fire under a crude lean-to. While reviewing their desperate situation, he told the group that this was not the end. He planned to send a hand-picked unit of fifty men to move ahead of the marchers to make contact with French-Canadian settlers along the Chaudiere River to purchase food. Arnold himself would lead a smaller flying unit to forge ahead to arrange the purchases. His enthusiasm gave the officers a renewed sense of hope.

Before setting off on his mission, Arnold had sent an order to the last division, led by Lieutenant Colonel Roger Enos, to hurry forward and divide their remaining food supplies with the starving marchers. Instead, Enos and his men had already voted to abandon the march and make their way back to Cambridge. The rest of the marchers were stunned by the news, seeing the decision as a betrayal. "May shame and guilt go with them," one of the soldiers wrote, "and whenever he seeks shelter may the hand of justice shut the door against him." 7.When Enos reached Cambridge, he was arrested and court-martialed; he was exonerated, however, because no one was there to testify that he had disobeyed orders.

The defection of Enos's three companies, and the few who had died, reduced Arnold's army to less than 800 men. Still, the marchers held on with remarkable determination, including the two women who had been allowed to accompany their husbands. Private John Henry, a rifleman, wrote about Mrs. Grier, the wife of a sergeant:

> Entering the pond . . . and breaking the ice here and there with the butts of our guns and feet, . . . we were soon waist deep in mud and water . . . [Henry searched for a better route] but the water in a trice cooling my armpits, made me gladly return into the file. Now Mrs. Grier had got before me. My mind was humbled, yet astonished, at the exertions of this good woman. Her clothes held more than waist high, she waded before me to firm ground. No one . . . dared to intimate a disrespectful idea of her. 8.

The other woman, Jemima Warner, was just as heroic. When her husband, Private James Warner, could go no further she remained behind with him until he died. With no shovel, she buried him as best she could in leaves and rocks. She then took up his musket and rushed ahead some twenty miles to catch up with the marchers.

Meantime, Arnold led the race for food to save his frozen, starving troops, traveling by canoe and leading sixteen men in four bateaux. After dashing ahead about forty miles, they reached the Chaudiere River, the last leg of their journey. But the river—*chaudiere* means "cauldron"—suddenly boiled into treacherous rock-filled rapids. All four bateaux were upset and two were smashed completely, losing their weapons and equipment.

Arnold and his men refused to give up. They wrung out their clothes and prepared to continue, when one of the men said he heard a waterfall. "Had we been carried over," Arnold wrote later in his diary, "we must inevitably been dashed to pieces and lost." 9. They survived the river and finally had the thrill of seeing the lights of settlers' cabins.

The French-Canadians welcomed the Americans with great enthusiasm. Within hours several tons of supplies were on the way, in canoes and overland. When the marchers saw cattle and horses coming through the forest, they thought at first it was a mirage; then, as Matthias Ogden wrote, "We realized we were blessed with the finest sight my eyes ever beheld." 10.

Private Abner Stocking described the condition of the marchers in the hours before they were saved:

> When we arose this morning many of the company were so weak that they could hardly stand. . . . When we attempted to march, they reeled about like drunken men, having now been without provisions five days. As I proceeded, I passed many sitting wholly drowned in sorrow, wishfully placing their eyes on everyone who passed by them, hoping for some relief. . . . My heart was ready to burst . . . when I witnessed distress which I could not relieve . . . 11.

For about fifty of the men, the help arrived too late. But Arnold's heroic mission had saved hundreds of lives.

The marchers, free of starvation, made their way through an icy marsh to the Chaudiere River. They followed the river's rugged downhill course through groves of cedar, hemlock, and spruce to the banks of the St. Lawrence River. Although bone weary, with tattered clothes hanging from their emaciated frames, they were thrilled by what they had accomplished.

Now, however, they faced new difficulties. First, they discovered the effects of Colonel Arnold's most serious mistake of judgment: part-way through the march, he had written to a friend living in Quebec. He entrusted the letter to an Indian courier who not only failed to deliver it but turned it over to a British officer. Thus alerted, the Quebec defenders now had two warships riding at anchor in the middle of the river, with several smaller boats patrolling up and down the river. The defenders had also seized or destroyed every canoe and small boat for miles on the invaders' side of the river.

Arnold was stunned to learn that their arrival was not a surprise. He had hoped to get across the river and meet up with the main army for a combined assault on Quebec before the city's defenses could be built up. Although he was disappointed, Benedict was as determined as ever. He would never admit defeat in any situation until he had done everything in his power to turn it into a victory.

While Arnold's men scoured the south shore of the St. Lawrence for canoes and small boats, Arnold had several days to study the stormy river and, on the opposite shore, the dark stone walls of the fortress city looming ominously from the top of a 300-foot cliff.

Now, in late November, he finally heard from the Schuyler army. That force, too, had been slowed from the start, first by weather and then by the defenders of St. Johns, who withstood the American siege for 42 days before they abandoned the town. During the siege, General Schuyler had been stricken with a painful illness and was forced to return to Albany. He was replaced by Brigadier General Richard Montgomery, a tall, handsome aristocrat, and a former officer in the British army, who was well-liked by the men and by his superiors.

Also during the siege of St. Johns, Ethan Allen, who had attached himself to the Schuyler-Montgomery army, thought he saw a chance to grab more glory. With a handful of followers, he slipped away from the siege and raced ahead in a brash attempt to capture Montreal. Instead, he found himself and his band surrounded by 400 British redcoats and their Indian allies. Forced to surrender, Allen spent more than two years in British prisons before being released in a prisoner exchange. Thus, at least one nemesis of Arnold's career was out of action for a time.

By the time the British gave up St. Johns, it was November, but from there General Montgomery's troops moved with speed. Sir Guy Carleton, Governor of British Canada and also the military commander, realized that the loss of St. Johns, placed Montreal and then Quebec in danger. He decided to give up on Montreal and race by the river to Quebec.

The American plan called for capturing Quebec before January 1, 1776, because on that date hundreds of militia enlistments expired, and it seemed likely that many would head for home. Although Montreal fell easily to the Patriots, it would be early December before Montgomery and Arnold could join forces. The quick fall of Montreal had allowed about 200 British defenders to reach Quebec before Montgomery. In a strange twist of fate, the Americans took Montreal so quickly in part because of the leadership of Colonel John Brown—Arnold's enemy from Ticonderoga days.

## Arnold's Heroism

At some point in the incredible march through the Maine wilderness, almost any other commander would have decided that the hardships were too great and turned back. But Arnold continued to push on with the gritty determination that saved the lives of his men. In the months that followed, Arnold was hailed for his heroic achievement. General Schuyler, in a letter to Congress, wrote that "Colonel Arnold's march does him great honor; some future historian will make it the subject of admiration to his readers." 12. James Warren called Arnold "a genius, who led a march under such circumstances, and attended with such difficulties that no modern story can equal." 13. He compared it to the famous historic march in the third century B.C. during Rome's war with Carthage, when the Carthaginian General Hannibal led his army (with some men riding elephants) through the snow-clogged Alps in order to attack Rome. Others picked up on the Hannibal image and began referring to Arnold as "America's Hannibal."

In a letter to Arnold, General Washington wrote, "My thanks are due, and sincerely offered to you, for your enterprising and persevering spirit." 14. He also offered him command of a regiment as a new army was formed for 1776. And, in a letter to Schuyler, Washington said, "The merit of this gentleman is certainly great, and I heartily wish that Fortune may distinguish him as one of her favourites. I am convinced that he will do every thing that prudence and valour shall suggest." 15.

While his new status as a hero was gratifying, Arnold was keenly aware that the praise was far from unanimous. As 1775 drew to a close, Congress showed no sign of promoting him to the rank of major general. In addition, his old enemies from the capture of Ticonderoga, including James Easton and John Brown, were still at work in their efforts to tear down his reputation.

The outcome of the battle for Quebec was soon to provide his detractors with more ammunition.

# CHAPTER FOUR

## Quebec—"The Forlorn Hope"

BENEDICT ARNOLD AND HIS RAGGED ARMY LEARNED that crossing the mile-wide St. Lawrence could be a daunting task. The weather remained bitterly cold, with frequent squalls of blinding snow. Two British warships were riding at anchor in the middle of the river, ready to blast any American boats—and their occupants—into small pieces. In addition, several patrol boats zigzagged up and down the river.

The Americans quietly began the crossing relays in about thirty birch-bark canoes and small boats on the moonless night of November 12, 1775. Arnold used experienced seamen to operate the canoes and boats. They guided their craft beneath the very gunwales of the warships and landed the troops in the shadow of the walled city.

After landing, the troops made their way part-way up the cliff, close to the lower city gates. As morning approached, 500 men had made the crossing. But an exchange of gunfire with a patrol boat persuaded Arnold to send a message to the 200 men still on the south bank to stay there and wait for another chance to make the crossing.

Morgan and other officers urged Arnold to launch a quick strike, taking advantage of surprise to capture the city before the defenders could organize. Arnold was sorely tempted to give the order, and several historians have said it might have worked; the British were badly disorganized, they were undermanned, and they lacked firm leadership. But Benedict did not dare risk it. If the surprise attack failed, it could ruin Washington's grand design for a two-army attack on the capital of British Canada. Reluctantly, he gave the order to climb to the top and set up a camp on the far side of the city.

While they waited for Montgomery's army to join them, Arnold's men found many of the French-Canadian residents to be friendly and helpful, especially while the money carried by Arnold held. A number of men acquired comfortable housing, and many were able to purchase clothing, shoes, and food, although there was little in the way of muskets or ammunition.

The Quebec defenders had seen Arnold's men soon after they arrived, and a sporadic exchange of gunfire began. The only artillery the Patriots had were a few small cannons they had managed to drag through the Maine wilderness, and these were useless against Quebec's thick stone walls. The most effective weapons the Americans did have were Dan Morgan's riflemen. With their long guns, they managed to pick off several wall-top sentries, enough to make the defenders a little uneasy.

Arnold realized that his army was far too weak to attack Quebec or even to start a siege. He figured that a force of at least 2,000 men and heavy artillery would be needed. Since his army consisted of only 500 men on the north side of the St. Lawrence, he could only hope that Montgomery could supply enough men and artillery to give the Americans a chance.

In the west, Montgomery's men moved easily into Montreal. Two days earlier, Governor Carleton had loaded his men and supplies on a flotilla of small boats for a race to Quebec. (Montgomery negotiated the surrender of Montreal, promising to pay fair prices for any supplies they took and to respect the people's religion.) Farther upriver at Sorel, American troops attacked Carleton's flotilla, forcing three boats to surrender and capturing the troops that had been defending Montreal. Guy Carleton managed to escape in a small boat and made his way to Quebec, where he assumed command of the city's defenses. He was confident the city could hold until the spring thaw when British ships could get through, bringing thousands of fresh troops.

Just before Carleton's return to Quebec, Arnold tried to lure the city's defenders into an open battle outside the walls, much as British general Wolfe had done to defeat Montcalm in the decisive battle of the Seven Years War (1756-1763). But the British simply scoffed at the challenge. In fact, when they saw the shabbily-dressed rebels, many without shoes, they laughed and jeered from the safety of their stone walls.

Benedict quickly realized his mistake and now feared that the enemy would attack the Americans. To avoid disaster, he ordered a night march on November 19, traveling twenty miles west where they set up camp at Pointe-aux-Trembles to wait for Montgomery. The march had been hard on the shivering soldiers, leading one of the shoeless Patriots to write, "We might have been tracked all the way by the blood from our shattered hoofs." 1.

By late November, the Americans learned that Montgomery's force was just thirty miles west of Pointe-aux-Trembles, bringing artillery and munitions, as well as plentiful supplies of clothing and guns. This was a happy interlude for Arnold's men, and they were able to bring the south bank detachment across the river.

Montgomery and Arnold finally met on December 1ˢᵗ, and from the beginning they got along well. Both were in their thirties, confident in their abilities, and neither was jealous of the other. Benedict seemed to get along well with officers who respected him such as Schuyler, Washington, and now Montgomery. Montgomery admired Arnold and, in a letter to Schuyler, noted that "he , , , is active, intelligent, and enterprising." And, of Arnold's wilderness marchers, he said, "There is a style of discipline among them, much superior to what I have been used to see in this campaign." 2.

The two generals were eager to capture Quebec, but they were keenly aware of what they were up against. Their combined forces numbered well under 1,500, about half the number defending Quebec. Several hundred Americans were suffering with smallpox, an often fatal disease, which many thought had been brought into the garrison by infected women sent by the Quebec defenders. In addition, some of the men whose enlistments were expiring had already started for home. Most of the militiamen were farmers or fishermen, many with families, and they were eager to be home to plant crops or prepare nets and boats for the spring. The men in both Arnold's and Montgomery's forces had already experienced the difficult enlistments and the winter weather in Canada did not promise improvement.

Arnold and Montgomery decided to test the possibilities of an assault on the city. They had their men build cannon emplacements out of ice and snow, hoping that an artillery bombardment would soften up Quebec's defenses. The attempt was a rather pathetic failure. Carleton had about 150 cannons available and he used the heaviest artillery to destroy the Americans' batteries, knocking them all out of action.

Montgomery and Arnold had one hope left: an assault on the city under cover of a nighttime blizzard. This decision caused some dissension among Arnold's men, especially in the company led by Captain Oliver Hanchet. Hanchet had already refused his commander's order to move supplies closer to Quebec's walls, insisting it was too dangerous. Normally, Arnold would have arrested Hanchet for such insubordination, but the army was so desperate for manpower that he had to tread lightly.

When Hanchet, supported by Brown and others, said he wanted to form an independent corps, separate from Arnold, Benedict was furious and humiliated, but knew he had to turn the matter over to Montgomery as commander of the combined armies. Montgomery used all the calm reasoning and persuasive skills that Arnold lacked to convince the officers and their men to stay with the assault and to continue to serve under Arnold.

Finally, on the night of December 30, the kind of fierce blizzard that Montgomery and Arnold had been waiting for moved in. With the wind picking up, the men quickly moved into position, now eager for action.

The American plan was for a two-pronged attack on the Lower Town near river level. Montgomery would lead his troops on the right flank, along the St. Lawrence, and Arnold on the left flank, along the Charles River. The two armies would then unite inside the walls and drive up into the Upper Town.

Arnold planned to spearhead the assault with a small force of hand-picked volunteers. He called this band the "Forlorn Hope." He was excited and bursting with energy. Once again, this was his dream—leading his men in a heroic attack on an enemy stronghold, pinning everything on a single throw of the dice. Victory would be momentous. Not just Quebec, but all of Canada could be in American hands. There would no longer be a danger of a British invasion from the north.

The bold American plan seems quixotic, and yet it might have succeeded. The fact that it seemed doomed from the start was due largely to bad luck.

Shortly after midnight on December 31st, two regiments of Canadian volunteers launched diversionary attacks, followed by the attacks of Montgomery's and Arnold's men. There was an immediate crash of cannons, mortars, rockets, and muskets, mixed with the steady beat of drums and the constant clang of church bells, the city's alarm system.

While Arnold led his men through deep snow past a row of brick warehouses, Montgomery made his way up a twisting path. He paused to wait for about 200 men to assemble, then led the way through a break in a barricade. At a distance of about forty paces, the British defenders managed to set off a single cannon loaded with grapeshot. The blast smashed into Montgomery and those closest to him, killing about ten instantly, the loss of their general and his two captains devastated the troops. With no one giving firm orders to continue, the assault turned into a disorganized retreat.

At the same time, Arnold led his men into a dark alleyway in the Lower Town, seeing little but the flash of muskets. They came to a barricade with two mounted guns. One gun fired, missing everything, but the other gun slammed a shell into Arnold's leg, knocking him to the ground. As he struggled to his feet, he shouted for his men to keep coming. But he could feel his boot filling with blood, he wrote later, and "the loss of blood rendered me very weak. . . . As the main body of troops came up, with some assistance I made my way to the hospital, near a mile on foot, being obliged to draw one leg after me, and a great part of the way under the continual fire of the enemy from the walls, at no greater distance than fifty yards. I providentially escaped, though several were shot down at my side." 3.

As Arnold painfully struggled to the rear, big Daniel Morgan assumed command. He ordered the men to use ladders to scale the barricades, and, to help them overcome their fear, he was the first to scramble over and leap into the town. For a few minutes Morgan and the men following him had remarkable success. They forced their way through street after street, taking scores of prisoners.

During a pause in the shooting, Morgan called a quick council of war. Many of his officers were missing, having lost their way in the storm and failing to find their way into the town. Morgan's men were on the edge of the Upper

Town and Morgan suggested that they press on. But his men disagreed, arguing that it was best to wait. They had more prisoners than men and, more important, Morgan later wrote, "General Montgomery was certainly coming down the river St. Lawrence and would join us in a few minutes, so that we were sure of conquest if we acted with caution. To these arguments," he concluded ruefully, "I sacrificed my own opinion and we lost the town." 4.

Morgan's assessment was right. Montgomery had already been killed and his troops, instead of battling toward Morgan, were in retreat. The British quickly recovered and battled back. They took control of houses around the Americans. Private George Morison described the beginning of the end:

> Our main body now appears, having taken a wrong route through narrow and crooked streets. . . . A furious discharge of musketry is let loose upon us from behind houses. In an instant we are assailed . . . by thrice our number. . . . [Ahead of us] the awful voice of Morgan is heard, whose gigantic stature and terrible appearance carries dismay among the foe wherever he comes. . . . They call on us to surrender, but we surrender them our bullets and retreat to the first battery. Here we maintain ourselves until ten o'clock [in the morning], when surrounded . . . many of our officers and men slain, and no hope of escape. We are reluctantly compelled to surrender . . . having fought manfully for three hours. 5.

Moments later, Morgan found himself surrounded and forced to surrender. With tears of frustration streaming down his face, he surrendered his sword to a priest rather than to a British officer. The battle for Quebec was over. Roughly one hundred Americans had been killed or wounded and four hundred taken prisoner.

In the hospital, Arnold learned of the battle's progress from the wounded men as they were brought in. He fully expected that Governor Carleton would soon attack but he refused requests to retreat. Instead, he remained in his bed armed with two pistols determined to kill as many as he could.

But Carleton did not attack. Instead, he was content to remain in the safety of the walled city and wait for the spring and the arrival of fresh British troops.

## Retreat, And . . .

From January to May, 1776, the situation in Canada remained uncertain. From the British perspective, Carleton held the remnants of the American army as prisoners, planning to take them aboard prison ships in the spring. Arnold and the Americans saw the matter quite differently. From their point of view, they were maintaining a siege of Quebec and would renew their assault as soon as they could. Arnold wrote frequently to Congress and General Washington, asking for reinforcements and for a healthy officer to take his place. In a letter to his sister, Arnold wrote, "I have no thought of leaving this proud town, until I first enter it in triumph. 6.

He continued to hope he could renew the assault on Quebec in the spring and occupy the city before the British reinforcements arrived. He was encouraged by the news that Congress had finally recognized the importance of Canada and new regiments were already on their way, traveling north on the Hudson-Champlain route.

The winter was slow to retreat, however, slowing the American relief regiments and making life miserable for Arnold and his men outside Quebec. Fierce blizzards were common and the temperature often stayed below -25 degrees F for days at a time. The Americans attempted to harass the defenders when work groups tried to collect firewood; a number of houses were burned down in the process.

On April 2, Major General David Wooster arrived from Montreal to replace Arnold who was still suffering from his leg wound, aggravated by a fall from his horse just as he was starting to ride again. Wooster, who was old and reportedly alcoholic, showed no interest in discussing his plans with Arnold, so Benedict headed for Montreal to complete his recovery.

Wooster failed badly in a matter of a few weeks, first in attempts to bombard the city from the Heights of Abraham. Governor Carleton's defenders simply returned the fire with more powerful artillery. When Wooster's plan to burn the British ships in the harbor also failed, he was replaced by General John Thomas.

Thomas quickly saw that the American siege was useless without more men and more artillery. He found that his command consisted of only 1,900 men, with less than half that number fit for duty. In the first days of May, Thomas learned that at least fifteen British ships were making their way through the breaking ice on the St. Lawrence River, carrying about 8,000 British regulars and German mercenaries. The new British force was led by two of England's most famous generals: John Burgoyne and Simon Fraser. The approach of these reinforcements effectively ended the American efforts to capture Quebec.

Governor Carleton, who had not once moved outside Quebec to attack Arnold's force, learned that the Americans were preparing to retreat and decided it was time to attack. With a band of 900, including the first 200 troops off the ships, the British and Canadians advanced against the American lines, where only 250 men were in condition to oppose them. When the Americans saw the size of the force attacking them, they panicked and fled, leaving 200 sick or wounded comrades. Carleton chose not to pursue the 250, but returned to the city to help organize the rest of the reinforcements.

By mid-May, there were more than 13,000 British at Quebec. Small brigades, numbering 400 to 700, set off to attack the few remaining Patriot strongholds in Canada.

At the same time, in Philadelphia, the delegates to Congress were beginning to consider the bold move of declaring independence. In May, all of the colonies were beginning to organize state governments as suggested by Congress. Over the next weeks of discussion about a declaration, there was a general feeling in Congress and among the Patriot population that the American forces in Canada were likely to succeed. In fact, in early June, while Congress was debating the first resolution for independence, General John Sullivan arrived at St. Johns, Canada, with a brigade of 3,300, and was joined by four regiments sent by Washington. The troops plus ample supplies of food, ammunition, and weapons seemed to indicate a new assault on Quebec. No one could have anticipated the disaster that was already destroying the American dream of conquering Canada.

### . . . Disaster

The beginning of the American defeat began in mid-May when a force of 400 was ordered to defend a stronghold called The Cedars, about 30 miles east of Montreal. But when a British force of 650 advanced toward them, the American major surrendered his entire garrison without a fight, even though a relief column was on the way from Montreal. In what was becoming a regular pattern for the Americans, the relief column of 100 under Major Henry Sherburne was surrounded only four miles from The Cedars and was forced to surrender.

Benedict Arnold had reached St. Johns when he learned of the American defeats. He immediately turned back to help, picking up fleeing soldiers on the way. The advancing British, which now included 500 Indians, heard of Arnold's approach; they sent a messenger to warn him that, if he attacked, the American prisoners would be turned over to the Indians. Arnold negotiated, agreed to take the American prisoners for later exchange, and returned to Montreal.

In early June, when General John Sullivan arrived at St. Johns with the large body of reinforcements, it looked as if the Americans could reverse the trend of disorganized flight and defeats. Sullivan was confident that he was just the man to lead the resurgence. His first move was to send 2,000 men in bateaux to attack a British stronghold at Trois Rivieres, about halfway between Montreal and Quebec.

The attack on Trois Rivieres turned into one more bungled defeat. Planning on a predawn surprise attack, the main force became lost and wandered into a swamp. These troops, under Anthony Wayne, managed to locate the fort and attacked, but fell back under heavy fire. The Americans scattered into the forest, hounded by Indians and Canadian volunteers. The battle cost at least 230 who surrendered and more than 400 dead or missing. British losses were fewer than twenty. Many of Sullivan's survivors made it to Sorel.

In Montreal, Benedict Arnold, who had learned that he had been promoted to brigadier general, recognized that their cause was hopeless. He led his 300 defenders out of the town and headed for St. Johns with the British pursuers closing in. At Sorel, General Sullivan reached a similar conclusion and ordered a retreat to Lake Champlain. He loaded his 2,500 men onto bateaux and fled ahead of the British fleet. As they retreated up the Richelieu River, they were pursued by more than 4,000 British regulars led by Generals Burgoyne and Fraser. The redcoats, one reported, were delighted to see "the rebels flying before us in the greatest Terror."

Arnold had sent the wounded and sick ahead to Ile aux Noix, but only two men could be spared to row each boat. This enabled the able-bodied to continue fighting a rearguard action. Arnold paused at Ile aux Noix, where Sullivan's force joined them. The Americans now numbered 8,000, but more than half were suffering from smallpox, malaria, or dysentery, as well as hunger, exhaustion, and the demoralization of defeat. Historian Richard Ketchum wrote, "The hand of death lay on this army, and everywhere men were crying out piteously for help." 7. A surgeon traveling with them said, "It broke my heart, and I wept till I had no more power to weep." 8.

Somehow, with Arnold's leadership, the battered Patriot army staggered south to Crown Point, and some to Ticonderoga. Men were dying of smallpox at the rate of ten to fifteen a day. A visiting chaplain wrote, "I did not look into a tent or hut [at Crown Point] in which I did not find either a dead or dying man." 9.

By the end of June, the question was: How long would Carleton and Burgoyne wait before assembling a fleet on Lake Champlain to launch an invasion of the American colonies? Such an invasion could end America's Revolution.

## Arnold: Pro and Con

The campaign for Canada had lasted only about nine months, beginning with Arnold's heroic march through the Maine wilderness and the Schuyler-Montgomery invasion on the Hudson-Champlain corridor. By the time the battered American army reached Crown Point and Ticonderoga, many Americans now saw the campaign as a humiliating disaster. When John Adams, a key leader in Congress, heard of the army's arrival at Crown Point, he wrote:

> Our army . . . is an object of wretchedness enough to fill a human mind with horror: disgraced, defeated, discontented, dispirited, diseased, naked, undisciplined, eaten up with vermin, no clothes, beds, blankets; no medicines, no victuals but salt pork and flour. . . . 10.

Of the roughly 5,200 who reached Crown Point, 2,800 required hospitalization; the rest, an observer wrote, were "emaciated and entirely broken down in strength, spirits, and discipline." 11.

What was Benedict Arnold's role in the mission's failure? A few weeks earlier, Congress had sent a committee of three highly respected men to try to find out why the campaign was failing. The three, headed by 70-year-old Benjamin Franklin, included Samuel Chase and Charles Carroll. After meeting with Arnold and others, Carroll offered this assessment of Arnold:

> Believe me, if this war continues, and Arnold should not be
> taken off pretty early, he will turn out to be a great man. He
> has great vivacity, perseverance, resources, intrepidity, and a
> cool judgment . . . 12.

Others had praise for Arnold, including the British. In a letter to General Burgoyne, for example, the British Secretary for American Affairs, wrote: "I am sorry Arnold escaped [from Canada] . . . I think he has shown himself the most enterprising man among the rebels." 13.

General Washington also recognized Arnold's achievements in Canada. He wrote to Congress, "The merit of this gentleman is certainly great; I heartily wish that fortune may distinguish him as one of her favorites." And in a note to Arnold the commander in chief wrote, "My thanks are due, and sincerely offered to you, for your enterprising and persevering spirit." 14. Congress rewarded him by promoting him to the rank of major general.

There were also critics of Arnold's role in Canada. His old enemies—John Brown, James Easton, and Moses Hazen—again went on the attack. All three had felt the sting of Arnold's criticism, especially regarding the mishandling of private property in Canada. Immediately after the retreat to Crown Point and Ticonderoga, the trio went to Philadelphia to present their charges against Arnold to Congress and to counter his charges against them. Arnold was 250 miles away at Ticonderoga and could not defend himself.

With so many charges against Arnold bombarding Congress, the delegates began to think there must be some truth to them. Brown's arguments seemed to be particularly persuasive. As Arnold's recent biographer James Kirby Martin has written: "Since Brown could say whatever he pleased [with Arnold unable to respond], he spewed out a scurrilous tale about Arnold operating as a notorious pillager in Canada, all of which, he promised, would soon be demonstrated. . . ." 15.

Angered by what was taking place, Samuel Chase wrote to Arnold, "I cannot but request all persons to suspend their opinion and to give you an opportunity of being heard," then added a warning, "Your best friends are not your countrymen."

Arnold was outraged when the decisions of the judges were announced in August, 1776. Nearly all of the charges against Brown, Easton, and Hazen were dropped. Brown and Easton received promotions as well as back pay to 1775. Hazen's case continued for several months, and the charges against Arnold also lingered until they were eventually dropped.

In Ticonderoga, Arnold received some solace from the announcement by General Horatio Gates, the new commander in the North, that Arnold would be in command of the defense of Lake Champlain. But he still felt that Congress had betrayed his patriotism and his service to his country, damaging his sense of honor. He confided his feelings to Horatio Gates: "I cannot but think it extremely cruel, when I have sacrificed my ease, health, and a great part of my private property, in the cause of my country, to be [vilified] as a robber and thief—at a time, too, when I have it not in my power to be heard in my own defense." 16.

From his first trip to Fort Ticonderoga in the spring of 1775 (with Ethan Allen) to his return with the battered American army little more than a year later, Benedict Arnold had been on a remarkable, thrill-packed journey. The cannons taken at Ticonderoga had been vital in enabling Washington's forces to drive the British out of Boston.

Then, in the extraordinary march through the uncharted wilderness of Maine, Arnold had displayed amazing courage, compassion, and leadership. His men knew they owed their lives to him and they became devoted to him for life. The attack on Quebec had failed, in large part because of Montgomery's death and his crippling wound at the very start of the fighting, but again he displayed extraordinary leadership and courage in getting the remnants of the army to the relative safety of Crown Point and Fort Ticonderoga.

In spite of his heroism, Arnold stirred up a hornet's nest of controversy and criticism. This hostility was partly caused by his own impatience with those who got in his way, especially officers who were not his superiors. In times of danger, when quick action or decisions were needed, Arnold had no equal. But when people like Brown or Easton crossed him, he became aggressive and arrogant, confident that he was right and anyone who didn't agree with him was an idiot or an enemy.

Those who opposed him often charged that he frequently stole property from merchants or enemy officers. There may have been some truth to these charges, although nothing was ever proved against him. Historians feel that Arnold's problem stemmed from his rush to act, leaving details about finances to be settled later. His viewpoint seemed to be that Congress—and other government agencies—should provide whatever the army needed; what amounts were to be repaid could be dealt with when the fighting was over. The question about Arnold's honesty and integrity continued until he committed his amazing act of treason.

In the autumn of 1776, Arnold was about to embark on one of his most incredible adventures. In fact, some historians feel this was Arnold's most heroic moment. All of his previous exploits had been as an army leader; his newest action was to be as a naval commander.

# CHAPTER FIVE

## _Meantime..._

IN THE EARLY MONTHS OF 1776, BENEDICT ARNOLD lay in a hospital outside Quebec, frustrated by his slow recovery from his leg wound, but still determined to maintain a siege of the city. At the same time, his influence on the war was being felt 200 miles away outside Boston. There, General George Washington, Commander-in-Chief of the Continental Army, was preparing for a showdown with the British occupying Boston.

The showdown turned out not to be necessary, in large part because of Benedict Arnold. Over the winter, General Seymour Knox arrived with fifty-seven cannons that had been hauled by ox-drawn sleds, struggling over snow-covered hills and icy streams from Fort Ticonderoga to Washington's headquarters at Cambridge. Working quietly and swiftly, Continental troops overnight positioned the cannons on the heights overlooking the city.

In the morning, the British in Boston were shocked to see dozens of cannons aimed at them. Rather than risk a bombardment, the British boarded ships and evacuated the city in March, 1776, sailing north to Canada. Washington, who was hailed as a hero for building up the army that helped force the evacuation, knew the British would be back. He began moving the army to New York City, figuring (rightly, as it turned out) that the British would strike there.

After the heady victory in liberating Boston in March, the rest of 1776 was a strange mixture of highs and lows, victories and defeats. In the spring, for example, the British hoped to achieve a quick victory in the South, planning to capture Charleston, South Carolina, where, they believed, Loyalists would rush to help the British. Instead, Patriots organized a powerful defense on Sullivan Island. Led by Colonel William Moultrie, the Southern militia crushed the attacking British and forced them to re-treat in late June, 1776. Two British warships lost about two hundred men, killed and wounded; American casualties were only twelve killed and twenty-four wounded. It would be more than two years before the British tried the South again.

At almost the same time, however, on June 29, a Patriot soldier looked out a second story window on New York's Staten Island and was stunned to see that "the whole bay was full of ships. I declare I thought all London was afloat." 1. By August, the British had landed 32,000 soldiers, supported by thirty warships, carrying 1,200 guns and 15,000 sailors.

To oppose this huge invasion force, Washington had only about 20,000 men, mostly half-trained militia; there was no naval support, and very little artillery. From late June on, the British redcoats advanced steadily across Long Island, Brooklyn, and Manhattan.

While the Patriots were winning in South Carolina and losing badly in New York City in the summer of 1776, Congress was meeting in Philadelphia to consider Thomas Jefferson's draft of the Declaration of Independence. On July 2, the declaration was approved, and the thirteen colonies became the Thirteen United States. Throughout July and August, the Declaration was read aloud and cheered in one community after another.

The Declaration of Independence gave Patriots a morale boost, but the army could not stop the British from crushing all opposition. Their warships were able to sail the rivers surrounding Manhattan, raking the streets with shells and bullets, and forcing the Patriots to retreat again and again. After New York City was abandoned, the British captured the forts and outposts along the Hudson River.

From September on, Washington spent four agonizing months trying to hold together his army while retreating across New Jersey with the British in pursuit. Finally, they crossed the Delaware River into Pennsylvania. By now, Washington's army had melted to fewer than 4,000 men. There had been many casualties, and others had gone home when their enlistments were up. Washington's strategy was simple: make sure there was always an army in the field; avoid a pitched battle at all costs because that could destroy his army.

In December, Washington was on the edge of despair. "I think the game is pretty near up," he wrote. 2.

But the game was not up. Both Washington and Arnold were about to display their respective genius in strategy and leadership.

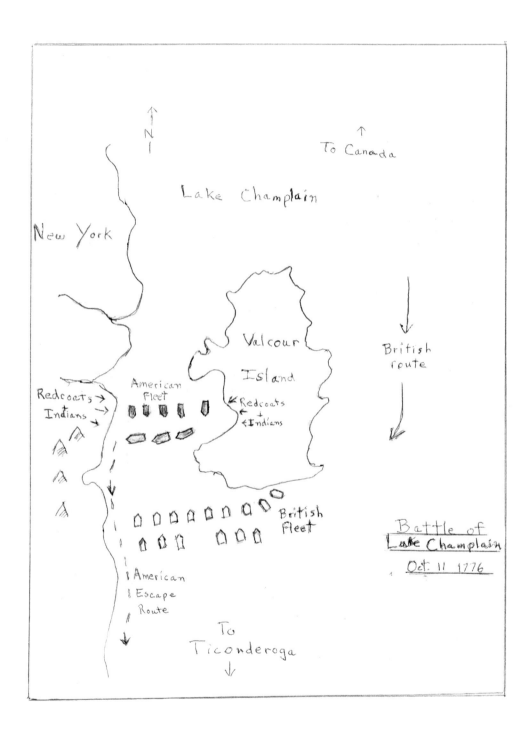

# CHAPTER SIX

# America's First Naval Hero

THE SUMMER OF 1776 WAS A BIZARRE AND HECTIC TIME for Benedict. With little time to recover from the disastrous retreat from Canada, he now had to prepare to fight a battle he knew he could not win, and he was to fight it, not on land, but on the waters of Lake Champlain. Adding to the difficulty was the fact that, when he was appointed to defend the lake, the Patriots had no navy on Champlain and very little time to build any kind of fleet. At the same time, he was once again hounded by his old enemies, leading to seemingly end-less legal battles. Somehow, Arnold's incredible energy, skill, and perseverance was to turn this chaos into one of his greatest adventures.

Arnold had no intention of backing down from the challenge. When General Horatio Gates appointed him to defend the lake, and told him to use his "courage and abilities [to prevent] the enemy's invasion of our country," 1. he was not exaggerating the importance of the event. The Americans knew that Guy Carleton was assembling a fleet in the northern part of the lake and, with an army of about 10,000 at his disposal, he could launch an invasion down the Champlain-Hudson corridor to Albany and wait there for another British force coming north on the Hudson River. New England would be cut off from the rest of the colonies, seriously threatening the Revolution.

The naval career of Benedict Arnold thus began in the summer of 1776 with the day-and-night effort to direct the building of some sort of fleet that might stop the British, or at least prevent them from invading before winter. From Skenesbouro, where initial construction took place, Arnold constantly bombarded Gates with requests for shipwrights, carpenters, woodsmen, blacksmiths, gunners, and seamen, as well as cannons, swivel guns, muskets, ammunition, clothing, blankets, and food. Then, at Ticonderoga, where each half-finished vessel was to be outfitted, Arnold and Gates sent out requests for items such as canvas, cordage, sail needles, white lead, and munitions.

## Legal Tangles

Throughout the summer's frenzied work, Arnold was almost constantly troubled by his enemies. Some of the questions and issues raised were to hound him up to the time of his treason.

A large portion of the troubles stemmed from the seizure of material from merchants and the British Army ordered by Arnold in the last desperate weeks in Canada. He had told the commissioners sent by Congress (Carroll and Chase; Franklin had already gone home) that his troops were in terrible shape. The commissioners authorized him to make the seizures in early June, 1776, for the use of the army. From that point, he kept the commissioners and his commanding generals informed of every step and every problem.

Trouble began when Arnold ordered Colonel Moses Hazen to take charge of the goods which had been piled on the banks of the St. Lawrence. Hazen refused, believing that Arnold had seized the materials for his own profit. Benedict roundly criticized Hazen who then asked for a court-martial to clear his name. A stormy court-martial followed, which included an irate Arnold close to challenging members of the court to duels. The matter was finally referred to Congress. (Months later Hazen was exonerated.)

The importance of the Hazen matter for Arnold was that members of Congress continued to wonder about his honesty and integrity. Others, notably James Easton and John Brown, both of whom had been poisonous thorns in Arnold's reputation, attacked him on issues involving enemy property.

Arnold had charged both Easton and Brown of plundering captured baggage of British officers. In April, 1776, Easton went to Congress to ask for permission to raise a regiment for Canada and for a court of inquiry to consider Arnold's charge against him. After some delay, Congress sent him to Canada to ask for such a court. By the time Easton got there, no one would talk to him because Americans were in frantic retreat.

That left the attacks on Benedict up to Brown. Congress acted in Brown's favor to the extent of confirming his rank and pay as a colonel in the Continental Army, retroactive to November 20, 1775. Congress also asked General Schuyler to establish a court of inquiry to clear Brown's name. Schuyler ordered General Gates to impanel a court. But Brown pushed his luck too far when he sent a formal complaint to Gates on September 3, saying that Benedict Arnold should be arrested for defamation of character.

Brown's complaint was filed during the last frantic days of Arnold's fleet-building. Benedict was so indispensable to the Patriot cause that Gates did not even consider arresting him and told Brown to go to the Board of War with his complaint. Brown backed down, deciding to wait until Arnold was not so important.

From early September, Benedict could devote his full attention to the approaching battle. The questions about him, however, would continue to hang in the air for the next three years, repeatedly threatening his reputation and his career. Samuel Chase, one of the commissioners to Canada, warned Arnold, "Your best friends are not your countrymen."2.

## The Battle

As the Battle of Lake Champlain approached, it was clear that no one was more important to the Patriot cause than Benedict Arnold. General Gates, for example, wrote to John Hancock at Congress that he was giving Arnold supreme command. "General Arnold," Gates explained, "(who is perfectly skilled in maritime affairs) has most nobly undertaken to command our fleet upon the Lake. With infinite satisfaction, I have committed the whole of that department to his care, convinced he will thereby add to that brilliant reputation he has so deservedly acquired." When Schuyler learned of this, he wrote that he was "extremely happy that General Arnold has taken command of the fleet. It has relieved me from very great anxiety under which I labored on that account." 3.

Both Gates and Arnold had thought Carleton might launch his attack in late September. They were pleased when the British were delayed into early October. Carleton had plenty of ships and artillery available but the larger ships had to be taken apart, carried past the rapids in the Richelieu River, then reassembled on Lake Champlain at St. Johns. This process gave Arnold a few extra days which were desperately needed.

By the end of September, Carleton had a strong fleet to win control of the lake. The ship *Inflexible*, for example, mounted eighteen 12-pounders, with more firepower than most of Arnold's vessels combined. The smaller *Maria* and *Carleton* were also powerful, and a slow-moving flatboat, the *Thunderer*, carried a number of 24-pounders—enough gun-metal weight to destroy the entire American fleet. The British also had twenty gunboats, one gun apiece, and four longboats, each with a howitzer. Carleton's fleet was augmented by crews and marines totaling nearly 2,000 as well as roughly 500 Indian warriors serving under British officers. The Indians traveled by canoe and could pose a constant threat from the shore and from islands.

Against this armada Arnold had hoped to have at least thirty vessels ready to face the British, but by early October, only seventeen were ready, and these were a mixture of styles, sizes, and firepower. Nine of the craft were *gundalows*—slow-moving vessels with a single mast and a fixed "sail" only with the wind; to move windward, the crew had to row. Each gundalow carried 45 men and had a fair amount of firepower—several light cannons and seven or eight swivel guns.

More valuable were three *row galleys*. These were about 75 feet in length, carried crews of 80 men, and were heavily armed, each having twelve cannons, including a 12- or 18-pounder in the bow, three or four 6-pounders along each side and two 9-pounders in the stern, as well as up to sixteen swivel guns. The row galleys were also maneuverable—each was equipped with two masts and triangular *lateen* sails capable of turning before the wind.

The rest of the fleet included a lightly-armed cutter, a sloop, and three schooners (captured earlier on the lake by Arnold): the *Liberty*, *Royal Savage*, and *Revenge*. The schooners were something of a cross between gundalows and row galleys. They were quite maneuverable with lateen sails. Each had a crew of about fifty, and carried several light cannons and swivel guns. All told, the Americans had about half the firepower of the British.

Arnold was disappointed in the small size of his fleet but he was even more disturbed by the lack of manpower, especially experienced sailors. In one of his desperate letters to Gates he pleaded for "one hundred good seamen as soon as possible; we have a wretched motley crew in the fleet. The marines, the refuse of every regiment, and the sailors, few of them ever wet with salt water—we are upwards of one hundred men short." 4. Arnold had little hope of finding one hundred skilled seamen; most seamen in coastal towns preferred to sign on privateers, which provided the hope for a share of profits in exchange for facing danger. He did have a total of nearly 800 men, although most had little training for fighting on a pitching wooden deck.

Although the odds were clearly against him, Arnold was determined to give the British a tough fight. He wrote of his confidence in the larger setting of the Revolution, saying that the cause of independence depended on a few Patriots being willing to take huge risks under "the protection of that Power upon whose mercy we place our hopes of freedom here, and of happiness hereafter." 5.

Benedict did have a few things in his favor: First, he knew that Carleton was more cautious than aggressive. The British commander clearly planned to take control of Lake Champlain and then capture the weakened American forces at Crown Point and Ticonderoga *before* the onset of winter. Arnold's fleet, therefore, did not have to defeat the British fleet, but rather to do enough damage, and to delay them long enough, to convince Carleton that he could not achieve his goals before winter; he would withdraw to Canada until the spring of 1777. That would give Gates and Washington six months to build up defenses at Ticonderoga and Crown Point.

A second factor in the Americans' favor was the possibility of surprise. In the hope of achieving that, Arnold designed an unusual battle plan and chose the location for putting it into action. The site he selected was the southern end of Valcour Island, a two-mile long, heavily-wooded island, rising 150 feet close to the New York shore. Arnold planned to place his fleet in the island's sheltered harbor, where they would not be visible to the British coming from the north until they had passed the inlet. Once they did spot the Americans, they would have to turn around, not an easy task since they had been traveling with a north wind and would now have to reverse direction and sail into the wind.

As the British made their turns, Arnold would send his best ships into the open water to start the battle, then retreat into Valcour harbor to join the rest of the flotilla in battle formation.

In the hope of improving his fleet's chances, Arnold decided to put on an act of bravado. He began boasting often and publicly that he intended to take the fight to the British, even attacking St. Johns inside Canada. He knew that spies would pick up these claims and report to Carleton. There was evidence that Arnold's ploy worked well enough to make Carleton more cautious. In late August, Arnold began sending squadrons of several ships to explore the lake, even in the north. Instead of challenging these incursions, Carleton moved his fleet closer into Canadian waters. He did not order the ships to start their advance south until October 6.

The extra time enabled Arnold to give his crews valuable sailing experience, as well as some gunnery practice, although lack of ammunition limited actual shooting. These weeks also gave Arnold ample time to display his leadership skills, and the men responded with steadily increasing confidence. They also had glimpses of his extraordinary courage. On August 26, for example, the ships were sailing easily southward when a furious storm, hidden by the hills, suddenly burst onto the fleet. Arnold ordered the captains to sail due south. One of the gundalows did not respond quickly enough and began drifting toward land and certain disaster.

Arnold saw the danger and responded instantly. He leaped into a small boat and ordered the oarsmen to row toward the troubled gundalow. The frightened men obeyed, rowing furiously through the towering waves until they were close enough for Arnold to stand up and shout through a speaking horn, directing the gundalow's captain how to lower the sail. It worked and the gundalow was saved. The men of the fleet had heard stories of their commander's fearlessness in the face of danger. Now they had seen it first-hand and they were beginning to see him as a leader they would follow anywhere.

The battle began much as Arnold had outlined it, and as it turned out, he also had luck on his side. On the morning of October 11, about 10 am, the Americans watched as the British fleet sailed past the island. Arnold had hoped that overconfidence in their power would convince the British that there was no need to send a scouting patrol. That's exactly what happened and the enemy fleet was two miles below Valcour Island before they spotted the Americans and began their turn into the wind.

From the raised quarterdeck of the *Congress* row galley, Commodore Arnold led the three row galleys out of their Valcour Island harbor and opened fire. The battle began in late morning and raged throughout the day. The air was filled with the almost constant roar of cannons, along with the crack of muskets and rattle of swivel guns. The din was mixed with shouted oaths and commands, the cries of the wounded, and the war whoops of Indians. Arnold rushed from cannon to cannon, often aiming the gun himself. Like other officers, his face, hands and uniform were black with gun powder. His shouts of directions and encouragement seemed to boost all the men's spirits.

After the initial exchange, Arnold ordered his row galleys back into Valcour's harbor to form a solid defensive line. One of the galleys maneuvered poorly and was badly shot up, eventually running aground. The Americans fought valiantly against the greater number and firepower of the enemy, suffering about fifty casualties and the loss of some ships. British losses were similar but they were better able to afford them.

The battle had been pretty much of a draw. However, as darkness approached and the shooting stopped, Carleton's fleet formed a solid barrier across the mouth of Valcour Bay. The British also had troops and Indian warriors swarming over the hills, including on Valcour Island. Although Arnold's men had done well, it was clear that they were now trapped. They could not possibly fight their way out in the morning. The British leaders were confident that they would force the rebels to surrender or destroy them.

Arnold and his officers decided it was better to risk a breakout and then try to race to the safety of Crown Point and Ticonderoga. Under cover of darkness and fog the Patriot ships moved out single file, with oars muffled, hugging the rocky New York coast. Arnold even had the wounded moved below decks so their moans or cries would not be heard by the British.

After several tense hours, the American flotilla was clear of the bay and began the race to Crown Point. In the morning, as the fog lifted, the stunned

British discovered that Valcour Bay was empty. Furious, Carleton ordered his fleet commanders to give chase. Crown Point was more than forty miles to the south, so he was confident they could catch up to the rebels.

The damaged American ships had trouble staying ahead. Three of the gundalows were so badly damaged that they had to be sunk. Arnold ordered one of the row galleys to lead the remaining nine vessels toward Crown Point, while the other two row galleys would try to delay the British. It was vital, Arnold told his captains, that at least a few ships got through; they would be proof that Carleton had not gained complete control of Lake Champlain.

After one row galley surrendered, the other, the *Congress*, commanded by Arnold, faced the British. He knew that the longer he and his men delayed the enemy, the better chance the remaining ships would have to reach Crown Point. For more than two hours, Arnold and his crew put up a brave fight against a total of seven enemy ships. Rather than surrender, Arnold made a sudden dash between two British ships, ran the *Congress* on shore and set it ablaze, rather than let the British capture it. That was a point of honor to him, and one that was widely praised.

Arnold and his crewmen raced on foot toward Crown Point. They caught up with five of his ships that had made it through. They boarded the row galley and sailed to Crown Point and then, on to Ticonderoga. It was a great triumph for Arnold and his men. But he and Gates were still fearful that Carleton was about to launch an attack on Crown Point and Ticonderoga.

Carleton, however, did not dare risk it. He had been surprised by the fighting ability of the rebels. Consequently, on November 2nd, he began withdrawing his ships to Canada, planning to launch a new invasion in the spring of 1777. In England, the king's ministers were not pleased. To them, it seemed impossible that a handful of rebel ships, led by the "horse jockey" Arnold, could battle a British fleet to a standstill. For the 1777 invasion, they wanted a man who was more willing to fight. They chose General John Burgoyne.

## Heroism Questioned . . .

When Arnold returned to Ticonderoga, he was treated as a hero. Gates, in his general orders for October 14, expressed thanks to "General Arnold, and the officers, seamen, and marines of the fleet for the gallant defense they made against the great superiority of the enemy's force. Such magnanimous behavior will establish the fame of American arms throughout the globe." 6.

In a letter to General Schuyler, Gates expressed his thanks that "it has pleased Providence to preserve General Arnold. Few men ever met with so many hairbreadth escapes in so short a space of time." The praise was echoed by members of Congress. Benjamin Rush wrote that "General Arnold . . . has conducted himself like a hero." Virginia's Richard Henry Lee praised all of Arnold's men: " . . . our people bravely maintained the unequal contest, conducting themselves with a valor that has extorted applause even from their enemies, and which certainly deserved a better fortune." 7.

The British added to the praise. A British officer who served in the Lake Champlain battle, wrote that the rebels' retreat "did great honor to General Arnold." And a popular British publication stated that "Arnold's desperate resistance [had greatly added to] that renown which he had acquired on land in the Canada expedition. He had not only acted the part of a brave soldier, but . . . also amply filled that of an able naval commander. . . . [Not even] the most experienced seamen could have found a greater variety of resources . . . to compensate for the want of force, than he did." The publication concluded that Arnold had "raised his character still higher than it was before with his countrymen." 8.

As always seemed to be the case, critics of Arnold emerged quickly. The main attack came from Brigadier General William Maxwell, who called Arnold "our evil genius to the north." He charged that Arnold must have used "a good deal of industry [to lose] our fine fleet [which] by all impartial accounts, was by far the strongest." 9.

At first, few people paid much attention to Maxwell's charges. But over the next several weeks, doubts emerged about Arnold's conduct. Some wondered if he had been serious when he boasted that he would carry the fight to the enemy, even invading Canadian territory. Was it possible, as James Wilkinson later charged, that the lake battle had taken place because of an "excess of rashness and folly [in order] to exalt his character for animal courage, on the blood of men equally brave." 10. James Wilkinson, who was to become one of the most notorious figures in American history, showed his tendency to advance his career by switching loyalties. As Arnold's aide during the retreat from Canada, he had nothing but praise for his general. Six months later, he had become Gates's aide and joined the chorus of Benedict Arnold's critics.

Although not many saw evil in Arnold's actions, a growing number wondered about his decision to fight at Valcour Bay; maybe, they thought, it would have been a better strategy to retreat to Crown Point or Ticonderoga and save the fleet. By November, then, Arnold's brilliant defense of Lake Champlain seemed much less heroic. Instead of acknowledging that his actions had convinced Carleton to withdraw to Canada, many in Congress now seemed to feel that his drive for personal glory led him to sacrifice men and ships. There was no one in the Congress willing to defend his honor. Even Richard Henry Lee, who had earlier praised him, now accused him of acting in a "fiery, hot, and impetuous" manner, instead of withdrawing in the face of a fleet "so much superior to his force." 11.

In later years, historians were more willing to recognize that Arnold's actions with his banged-together ships, were actually crucial to the future success of the Patriots' cause. The famous naval historian Alfred Thayer Mahan wrote in the late 19th century that the Americans were strong enough to force the British to surrender at the Battle of Saratoga because of " . . . the invaluable delay secured to them by their little navy on Lake Champlain created by the indomitable energy, and handled with the indomitable courage of the traitor Benedict Arnold." He added, "Never had any force, big or small, lived to better purpose or died more gloriously . . ." 12.

In the following months, Arnold had new chances to prove his courage and leadership.

CHAPTER SEVEN

# Heroics And Politics

By early 1777, less than two years after the start of America's Revolution, Benedict Arnold had become one of the Patriots' most heroic figures. People praised his many exploits, which included: acquiring the vital artillery from Ticonderoga and St. Johns; risking starvation and death in the almost mythical march through the Maine wilderness; exercising gritty leadership in the battle for Quebec; and performing extraordinary feats on Lake Champlain.

At the same time, however, some Americans—including leading members of Congress—saw him as dangerous and untrustworthy. His critics, including Easton, Brown, and Hazen, attacked him relentlessly in newspapers and in Congress. Several of the charges, including shady financial dealings, tended to stick, even though proofs were lacking or questionable. Several members of Congress developed an abiding distrust of Arnold. Some felt that the repeated accusations were likely to have some validity.

General Washington was keenly aware of Congressional uneasiness regarding Arnold. He also knew that nearly all members of Congress were determined to maintain firm civilian control over the military. They didn't want Arnold—or Washington for that matter—to become too popular. A military dictatorship would quickly end the Patriot cause.

After the Battle of Lake Champlain, Arnold saw little action for the next six months. He rested at Ticonderoga for a few days and prepared to go to New Haven to see his three sons and his sister Hannah for the first time in nearly a year and a half. The plan changed suddenly when Gates received an urgent plea for help from General Washington in Pennsylvania. General Gates organized eight regiments of Continental Army troops and headed south. Arnold joined them, then raced ahead to reach Washington's headquarters on the Delaware River in mid-December.

Washington told Arnold about his plan to recross the Delaware and attack Britain's hired allies—the Hessians—stationed at Trenton, New Jersey. Arnold, of course, was eager to be part of the surprise attack, especially after the months of losses and retreats that Washington's army had experienced. Washington, however, had other plans for his fighting general. He asked Arnold to hurry to New England where a British force of about 7,000 had landed at Newport, Rhode Island. The commander-in-chief wanted him to rally Patriot militia to prevent British forces from moving inland.

Enthusiasm for the Patriot cause had dipped badly during the months of military disasters. The one bright spot had been Arnold's heroism on Lake Champlain. Washington hoped that Benedict's presence in New England would encourage more militiamen to sign up. Arnold immediately headed north.

He stopped in New Haven for a few days, basking in the affection of his three sons and his sister Hannah. The oldest boy, Benedict, was about to turn nine, Richard was seven and Henry was four. Benedict was also pleased by the warm reception he received from the people of New Haven, who were thrilled by his courageous defense on Lake Champlain. When he left for Providence, he was accompanied by the same warm response of people for the entire journey.

In Rhode Island, he found that the British were in firm control of Newport and the surrounding area. American General John Spencer had fewer than 5,000 half-trained militia to try to hold them at bay. While Arnold was eager to develop a plan for dislodging the British, he knew he needed more men to have a chance.

From his arrival at Providence on January 12, until the end of the month, he had little success recruiting militia. He wrote to Washington with a description of his battle plan, and added that, because of the lack of troops, "I believe your Excellency will not think it prudent for us to make a general attack." 1. Washington quickly responded, saying that no attack should be attempted unless there was "certainty of success."

Arnold was deeply disappointed to learn that his role in Rhode Island was to be defensive, with little chance for combat. Even the defensive posture seemed less demanding when the Americans learned that Sir Henry Clinton, the British commander, did not intend to attack Providence. Instead, he had decided to go into winter quarters at Newport. In fact, Clinton had received permission to spend the winter in England.

Spencer and Arnold agreed that Benedict should go to Boston to try to raise three or four regiments of Continental troops, rather than militia. On his journey, he learned about three of his old friends—Daniel Morgan, Eleazer Oswald, and John Lamb—who had been captured at Quebec. In November, Arnold had asked General Washington to see if he could speed their release in a prisoner exchange. The exchange was completed and all three were already rebuilding their military careers. Oswald, who rode with Arnold on the way to Boston, told him that Morgan was organizing a new regiment of Virginia riflemen; John Lamb, who had survived a disfiguring face wound, had been promoted and given orders to organize the Continental Army's 2nd Artillery Regiment. Congress, however, had provided no funds for cannons, horses, and other materials. Lamb used his own money and borrowed more, but he was still well short. Arnold sent word through Oswald, who was to be an officer in the new regiment, for Lamb to go to Hannah Arnold to receive a note for 1,000 pounds.

That act of generosity was typical of Benedict's attitude about money. He knew he might not be repaid by John Lamb, but as long as he had the money, that was how he wanted to use it.

### Arnold's Romantic Interlude

In Boston, Benedict wanted to make a good impression, so he contacted an old acquaintance, Paul Revere, for help in selecting the best uniform accoutrements. One reason for the sartorial splendor was that he had met a pretty young Bostonian named Elizabeth "Betsy" De Blois. Benedict enlisted the aid of Lucy Knox, wife of General Henry Knox, Washington's over-sized artillery officer. Arnold, in a letter to Lucy, asked her to arrange the delivery of a trunk of gowns to the "heavenly Miss De Blois."

Benedict's gift showed a remarkable lack of taste. The dresses had been confiscated from an enemy shipment, but even if delivered in person, they would not have constituted a sophisticated offering. Perhaps not surprisingly, Miss De Blois refused the gift and did not encourage further overtures by the impetuous general. Arnold left Boston a loser in love and with few new recruits.

Arnold had little time to fret over his failure to win the hand of Miss De Blois. In early March, 1777, he received a letter from Washington with crushing news: Congress had voted to promote five men to the rank of major general. All five had less experience than Arnold and none had shown anything approaching his ability. But all five were now his superiors and he became the oldest remaining brigadier general. This news was a blow to Benedict's pride that some biographers feel he never recovered from.

Washington had not been consulted by Congress in the choices made, and he was stunned to see no mention of Benedict Arnold. In his letter to Arnold, he cautioned him not to "take any hasty steps" until the matter could be looked into. Washington also wrote privately to his friend in Congress Richard Henry Lee, saying he was

> anxious to know whether General Arnold's non-promotion was owing to accident or design, and the cause of it. Surely a more active, a more spirited, and sensible officer, fills no department of your army. Not seeing him then in the list of major generals, and no mention made of him, has given me uneasiness, as it is not to be presumed (being the oldest brigadier) that he will continue in service under such a slight. 2.

Arnold was both shocked and hurt by the news of his non-promotion. On March 14 he wrote to Washington that he thought the action by Congress was "a very civil way of requesting my resignation, as unqualified for the office I hold. . . . When I entered the service of my country my character was unimpeached. I have sacrificed my interest, ease and happiness in her cause. . . ." He added that he wanted a court of inquiry into his conduct, but in deference to Washington's request, "I shall certainly avoid any hasty step . . . that may tend to the injury of my country." 3.

Washington continued to be troubled by what was happening to Arnold.

But he was keenly aware that Congress had become very touchy in their dealings with the military's officers, especially generals, convinced that civilian government had to keep tight control over its officers, including Benedict Arnold and even George Washington. Knowing this, Washington still turned again to his friend Lee. "I could wish to see Arnold promoted to the rank of major general," he wrote, "and that he should be given seniority over the others. It is by men of [Arnold's] activity and spirit the cause is to be supported." 4.

What neither Washington nor Arnold knew was that the enemies of both men were becoming more bold. The winter of 1776-1777 provided severe tests for both men.

### Enemies Old and New

About the time that Arnold learned of his non-promotion, he also learned that one of his old enemies—John Brown—had submitted a petition to Congress. Brown listed thirteen "crimes" Arnold had committed and urged Congress to arrest and court-martial him. Brown also attacked Arnold for his "unjustifiable, false, wicked, and malicious accusation" that Brown had stolen property at Ticonderoga. 5. "Money is this man's god," the petition concluded, "and to get enough of it he would sacrifice his country." 6.

One of several facts that Arnold was not yet aware of was that the petition had been delivered to Congress by General Gates—the man who had worked closely with Arnold through the Lake Champlain crisis and praised him for his heroic actions, and who had then rushed south to aid Washington.

Instead of rushing to meet Washington, however, Gates suddenly slowed down. Washington was upset, particularly because another general he had counted on—General Charles Lee—was also inexplicably slow.

What had gone wrong, especially with Gates? Why did he so suddenly seem to turn against both Arnold and Washington?

The answer was that both Gates and Lee had come to think of Washington as an inept bungler. They believed that his mismanagement had enabled the British to take control of New York City and then sweep across New Jersey, nearly destroying the remnants of Washington's army. When the commander-in-chief ordered the two generals to move with speed, they simply refused. Both Gates and Lee were now so intent on advancing their own careers, they didn't care about endangering the Revolution.

Lee was so slow that a British force caught up with him and captured him. Major General John Sullivan took command of his 2,000 troops and quickly had them across the Delaware with Washington.

When Gates finally arrived in camp, he immediately argued with Washington about the commander's plan for a secret attack on Trenton. Gates insisted the Patriots should move deeper into Pennsylvania. Washington would not listen, so Gates, claiming illness, left and went to Baltimore where Congress had relocated. There he met with friends in Congress, seeking their support to have him replace Schuyler in the Northern District. His eventual goal was to replace Washington as commander-in-chief.

It was in Baltimore that Gates delivered Brown's anti-Arnold petition to Congress. Gates had apparently been troubled by the public acclaim Arnold had received after Lake Champlain. He now viewed the naval hero as a rival for power, not an ally. By early 1777, Gates seemed determined to destroy Arnold's career.

### Battlefield Heroics . . . Again

Since the British showed no sign of moving inland, Arnold felt it was safe for him to return to New Haven, spend some time with his family, and prepare to go to Philadelphia to try to clear his name with Congress. The day before he was to leave, a courier arrived with the news that a British force had landed at Norwalk, Connecticut and was marching toward Danbury where the Patriots had a major supply depot. Arnold immediately headed for Danbury.

Benedict rode swiftly but stopped long enough at every town for militiamen to join him to defend Connecticut from British invaders. He hoped for an outpouring of citizen soldiers, something like the thousands who had answered the call at Lexington and Concord, and then at Bunker Hill. But only about 100 followed him, including Brigadier General David Wooster, a New Haven neighbor, and briefly the commander outside Quebec.

At the town of Redding he met militia general Gold S. Silliman in command of about 500 men. Silliman told him that earlier in the day, a force of 2,000 British had taken Danbury without opposition. The redcoats had destroyed tons of supplies and weapons, then torched the town, leveling nearly every house. The British, under the command of William Tryon, the former Loyalist governor of Connecticut, headed for the coast, planning to board their ships before the Patriots could organize any opposition.

Arnold was well aware that his militia force, which numbered less than 600 and with little training, were no match for the invaders, but he was determined to show that Americans would defend their lands. He divided his little army, having Wooster harass them from the rear, while he and Silliman raced cross-country to Ridgefield, where they planned to block the road to the coast.

When Wooster caught up to the British and opened fire, Tryon stopped instantly and ordered a full-scale counter-attack, supported by the fire from six field cannons. The Patriot militia panicked and fled. Wooster was seriously wounded; his son rushed to help him. When a redcoat ordered the younger Wooster to surrender, he refused and the redcoat ran him through with a a bayonet, killing him instantly. David Wooster died a few days later.

Wooster's attack did gain valuable time, allowing Arnold and Silliman to lead their men cross-country to Ridgefield, where they set up a barricade of logs, rocks, and overturned wagons. Quietly urging his men to remain calm, Arnold rode back and forth behind the defense.

The British appeared in mid-afternoon and Tryon immediately ordered an attack. The frightened Americans, outnumbered about 20 to 3, held their line. Surprised by the Patriots' stubborn defense, Tryon ordered a flanking attack. Being attacked from two sides was too much for the American militiamen. They faltered, then started to run.

Arnold ordered a retreat. In his diary, he described the action that followed:

> [I] turned my horse to retreat just as General Agnew's infantry, running down the hill from the rocks, fired a complete round at my humble person. The Lord knows why I was not killed, nine bullets went through my poor horse, which fell

dead at once, and my feet were entangled in the stirrups, but I was not wounded.

'Surrender, you are my prisoner,' cried a grenadier, as he rushed forward with a fixed bayonet to run me through. 'Not yet,' I remarked; and this little interchange of conversation had given me time to draw a pistol from its holster with which I shot the soldier dead. 7.

The day's fighting was over. The British had suffered heavy losses, so Tryon decided to pause for the night, rather than risk marching fifteen miles to the coast in the dark. Arnold spent the night riding the countryside, urging militia to join him in fighting the invading British.

Once again, few militia joined him by morning. Both Arnold and Washington were increasingly disturbed by the unwillingness of the American people to defend their homes and the Patriot cause. Washington called it a "langor [*sic*] that prevails everywhere." 8. Arnold, a delegate for Congress said, could not understand how the people of Connecticut could put up with "such an insult without resistance or proper revenge." And Arnold himself said of the citizen-soldiers, "I wish never to see another of them in action." 9.

In spite of the problems, Arnold was still ready to fight. As the British neared the coast, he had his men use hit-and-run tactics, since they were too badly outnumbered for a direct attack. Arnold was again in the thick of the fighting, riding along the line, urging the militia to stay steady. A surprised witness wrote that he "exhibited the greatest marks of bravery, coolness, and fortitude . . . ignoring the enemy's fire of musketry and grape shot." 10.

In a climax that echoed the Ridgefield encounter, Arnold's horse was hit and crumbled to the ground, but this time Arnold was thrown clear, although a musket ball tore through the collar of his coat. Seeing their commander down was too much for the Connecticut militiamen. They broke and ran, giving the British a clear path to their ships waiting off the coast.

Once again, even the British praised Arnold, calling him "a devilish fighting fellow." 11. The members of Congress did an about-face and immediately promoted him to the rank of major general on May 2. While that move was welcome, the delegates did not address the matter of seniority, so the other five major generals still outranked him.

John Adams, who would become the nation's second president, had an unusual idea for honoring Arnold's heroic stand. He wanted to have a medal created, much as Congress had done to honor Washington for the liberation of Boston. Adams thought that such a medal would encourage men to enlist in the Continental Army. He described the medal:

> . . . I wish we could make a beginning, by striking a medal with a platoon firing at General Arnold, on horseback, his horse falling dead under him and he deliberately disentangling his feet from the stirrups and taking his pistols out of his holsters before his retreat.

On the reverse, the medal would show Arnold "mounted on a fresh horse, receiving another discharge of musketry, with a wound in the neck of his horse. . . ." 12.Adams was convinced that people had not seen such examples of outstanding bravery on the battlefield.

## Matters of Honor

Congress never acted on Adams's idea of a medal honoring Benedict Arnold, largely because there were so many doubts about his character. (In addition to the medal struck for Washington in 1776, seven others were created during the Revolution.)

Arnold knew nothing about the idea of a medal, but he was still deeply troubled by the failure of Congress to establish his seniority over the other five major generals. He was also troubled by the notion that neither General Gates nor Washington seemed to be granting him whole-hearted support.

Eager to find out where he stood, Arnold left New Haven and rode to Washington's new headquarters in Morristown. He didn't realize how much Washington admired him. The commander-in-chief warned friends in Congress that no general was likely to remain in service after losing his seniority to less qualified men. He always advised his young general to be patient and bide his time. But when Arnold arrived unexpectedly and showed him the petition

Brown had sent to Congress, Washington changed his mind and encouraged him to go to Congress. He realized that Congress was not behaving honorably in their treatment of Arnold.

The members of Congress greeted him warmly and presented him with a fine horse to replace the two he had lost. While they put off discussing the problem of seniority, they did appoint a committee—the Board of War—to consider his claim for expenses in the Quebec campaign. The board's statement declared "entire satisfaction . . . concerning the general's character and conduct, so cruelly and groundlessly [attacked in John Brown's] publication." 13.

Arnold was still seething over the matter of seniority. He wondered if Congress was trying to quiet him with the gift of a horse. But he was reluctant to resign and leave the army. He loved the excitement of battle. He knew that he had no equal in assessing a military situation, making a quick strategic decision, and inspiring his men to do whatever he asked. He was also convinced that his military career offered the best hope of restoring his family's honor and wealth.

Over the next few weeks, however, he observed that his friend and mentor, General Philip Schuyler, was struggling with enemies in Congress to hold onto his position as head of the Northern Military District. And he watched General Horatio Gates, his former friend and ally, turn against Schuyler, against Arnold himself, and even against Washington.

If so much depended on the whims of Congress, what chance did Arnold have, especially since he lacked political allies? Consequently, on July 10, 1777, Arnold reluctantly wrote a letter of resignation to Congress. He explained that he did not resign his commission out of "a spirit of resentment (though my feelings are deeply wounded), but because of a real conviction that it is not in my power to serve my country in the present rank I hold." Not advancing him above the other major generals was, he wrote, an "implied impeachment of my character and declaration of Congress that they thought me unqualified for the post that fell to me in the common line of promotions." 14

Arnold handed in the resignation and prepared to leave Philadelphia. He assumed his military career had ended but once again, fate intervened and changed his plans.

While Arnold was still in Philadelphia, Washington received two stunning reports: First, General Howe had loaded 15,000 troops on 260 transport ships. Was he planning to move south to attack Washington's 7,500-man army? Or, would he move north, up the Hudson to connect with the British moving south from Canada? Either move could be disastrous for the Patriot cause.

The other report was that the British in Canada, now under General Burgoyne, had launched their invasion down the Champlain-Hudson corridor. With more than 10,000 men, including German mercenaries and Indians, Burgoyne's force could easily overwhelm the Patriot army under Schuyler, based at Albany. General Arthur St. Clair who was supposed to defend Ticonderoga, took one look at the approaching British and abandoned the fort on July 5 without firing a shot. Burgoyne had now paused at Skenesboro to wait for supplies before making his final push for Albany.

On July 10, Washington asked Congress for 6,000 new troops and Congress, finally realizing that the Revolution was in danger, readily agreed. Congress also agreed when Washington requested that Benedict Arnold be sent north to train these recruits. In making the request, Washington revealed how highly he regarded the hero of Champlain and Danbury. He pointed out that Arnold ". . . is active, judicious, and brave, and an officer in whom the militia will repose great confidence." 15.

Congress managed the matter of Arnold's resignation by simply ignoring it. Arnold was understandably delighted that he was still in uniform and was being sent to the likely locale of the next important fighting. The approaching battles, in fact, would turn out to be the turning point of the American Revolution. And once again, Benedict Arnold was to play a pivotal role.

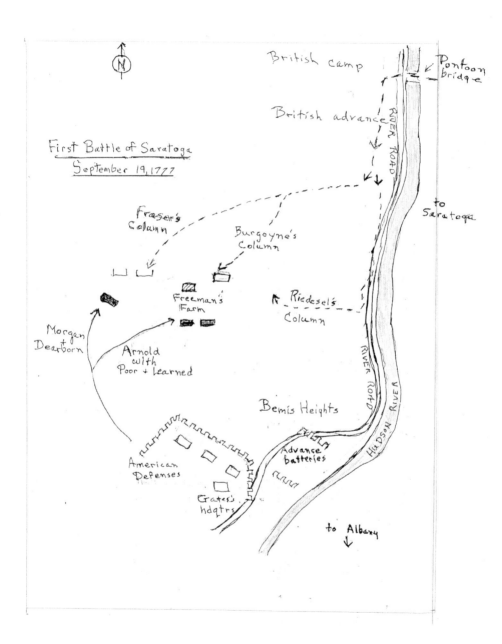

First Battle of Saratoga
September 19, 1777

British camp

Pontoon bridge

British advance

RIVER ROAD

to Saratoga

Fraser's Column

Burgoyne's Column

Riedesel's Column

Freeman's Farm

Morgan
Dearborn

Arnold
with
Poor + Learned

Bemis Heights

RIVER ROAD

HUDSON RIVER

Advance batteries

American Defenses

Gates's hdqtrs

to Albany

# Chapter Eight

# The Battle of Saratoga, Part 1

In June, 1777, British General John Burgoyne led his 10,000-man invasion force south from Canada on the Lake Champlain-Hudson River corridor. His army looked invincible, and "Gentleman Johnny" was brimming with confidence. He was a dashing figure, an actor, a playwright and a hero of the Seven Years' War (1756-1763), immensely popular with his troops and with the government leaders in London.

As the long procession of soldiers, horses, oxen, wagons, and field artillery rumbled south, along with scores of supply boats following on the lake and river, the commanding officers were sure they would easily smash through the American defenses to Albany. There they would meet General Howe's army coming north from New York City and a third, smaller army under Colonel Barry St. Leger coming east along the Mohawk River.

In the beginning, the British and their Hessian allies moved swiftly. On July 5, they took Fort Ticonderoga, one of the keys to American defenses. The fort's defenders, commanded by Major General Arthur St. Clair, fled without firing a shot. With the enemy close behind, St. Clair's men made a torturous retreat through rugged, wooded hills, losing nearly 400 men (killed, wounded, or captured) in a running battle to Fort Edward. Although the Patriots managed to strike back several times, inflicting fairly heavy casualties, the loss of the fort and the scattering of St. Clair's men, constituted a devastating defeat for the American cause.

Burgoyne now paused at Skenesboro to wait for supplies from Canada. The delay stretched out to three weeks. No one could see it yet, but the long wait revealed several weaknesses in the British invasion. One serious problem was the time needed to move a huge army through the dense wilderness of the Hudson River Valley. Burgoyne had allowed many of his officers to bring their wives, and some also brought their children. This slowed down the army's movements and added to the logistical problems of transporting food, as well as weapons, 138 pieces of field artillery, and ammunition.

Another weakness emerged from Burgoyne's personality. He was enjoying himself and felt no need to rush. Baroness von Riedesel, wife of the general who commanded the Hessians, wrote in her diary that Burgoyne was ". . . having a jolly time, spending half the night singing and drinking and amusing himself with the wife of a commissary, who was his mistress and, like him, loved champagne." 1.

During the three-week lull, Arnold received his orders from General Washington, headed north, and reached Fort Edward on July 22. He met with Schuyler and helped him plan defense strategies. Their greatest worry was being short of troops. Few volunteers had answered Schuyler's repeated appeals for militia that he sent throughout New England and New York. He was also troubled by the news that another British force was moving east across New York state. With too few men, he wrote, "I am to face a powerful enemy from the north, flushed with success, and pressed at the same time from the west." 2.

When the British and Hessians neared Fort Edward in late July, Schuyler had no choice but to retreat closer to Albany. Burgoyne now felt that finishing off the rebels would be quick and easy. He sent glowing reports to London, where he was hailed as a conquering hero. He issued a proclamation, calling on the rebels to surrender, or else . . . Major General Friedrich von Riedesel, commander of the Hessians, echoed that confidence, saying that Burgoyne's campaign would be a "march of annihilation."

Schuyler did what he could with the time gained by Burgoyne's delay. He sent several hundred woodsmen into the thick forests, where they cut down trees to block pathways, destroyed bridges, and rolled boulders into streams to make passage difficult. When the British resumed their march, they could not advance more than a mile a day. As the work crews struggled forward, the Americans could hear the thud of their axes in their effort to rebuild more than thirty bridges. Arnold was sent ahead with a squad of soldiers to harass the enemy column so they could attack it at weak points.

The planning and energy poured into these efforts began to pay off. In fact, the work of Schuyler and Arnold made it possible for the Patriots to put up a strong defense. Their efforts were helped by other developments. General Washington, for example, could not spare much man power, but he did send Colonel Daniel Morgan and his regiment of riflemen, knowing how well Morgan and Arnold had worked together in the Quebec campaign. He also sent General John Glover's Marblehead seamen who had ferried Washington across the Delaware the previous December.

Two other developments involved Burgoyne's flanks—first on the left flank, then on his right.

### Burgoyne: Storm Clouds On His Left

While Burgoyne waited for supply wagons to arrive from Canada, he also was in desperate need of horses, cattle, and oxen. Scouts told him there were large numbers of animals in the Hampshire Grants (Vermont) and that many of the people were loyalists who would be eager to welcome the British and Hessians. This sounded like easy pickings to Burgoyne, so in mid-August, he sent a force of about 600 Hessians, British, and Indians, all under the command of German Lieutenant Colonel Friedrick Baum, toward Bennington (Vermont) to round up as many animals as possible.

Neither Burgoyne nor Riedesel worried about the militia under Seth Warner, since they had retreated into northern Vermont. But they did not count on the extraordinary abilities of John Stark. Like Benedict Arnold, Stark had been passed over for promotion by Congress. He went home to Vermont, and became a general of militia. When he learned that Baum's force was coming, he managed to raise 1,500 militiamen in less than a week. And Seth Warner, with about 300 men, promised to meet Stark at Bennington.

When Baum saw some of Stark's men approaching, he paused on a hill and prepared to greet the men he assumed were loyalists, coming to join them. Too late, he realized the truth as Stark's men burst from the woods and attacked from all sides. Baum's force was saved from total disaster only by their hilltop location and the approach of 550 additional men sent by a worried Riedesel. The enemy force was soon overwhelmed, however, especially after a shell hit an ammunition wagon causing a tremendous explosion. Stark's men rushed up the hill and used sabers, bayonets, and butts of their muskets to destroy Baum's force. The Indians fled, but hundreds of Hessians and British were cut down or forced to surrender. The arrival of Seth Warner's militia helped crush most of the 550 Hessian reinforcements.

The Battle of Bennington was a stunning victory for the Patriots. The American casualties were light, while the British and Hessians lost roughly 800 men, killed, wounded, or taken prisoner. That number amounted to nearly ten percent of Burgoyne's invasion force. In a report to London, Burgoyne wrote that the population of Vermont was "the most active and most rebellious race on the continent, and hangs like a gathering storm on my left." 3.

Burgoyne consoled himself with the knowledge that Colonel St. Leger was at Oswego in New York State and would soon be arriving on the Hudson. He did not yet know that St. Leger had also run into trouble. In his case, the trouble was Benedict Arnold.

### . . . And On His Right

British Lieutenant Barry St. Leger led an expedition of nearly 1,000 British, Hessian, and Loyalist troops from Montreal to Oswego, New York, There, on July 25, they were joined by about 1,000 Iroquois warriors led by a remarkable man named Thayendanegea, or Joseph Brant. Brant had lived among whites for many years and had served as secretary to Guy Johnson, the British Superintendent of Indian Affiars. (Johnson had helped persuade most of the Iroquois nations to side with the British throughout the American Revolution.)

Confident of success, St. Leger led his army of 2,000 men toward Albany. The only obstacle in his path was Fort Stanwix on the Mohawk River. The fort was held by about 750 men commanded by Colonel Peter Ganesvoort. They were restoring the fort and planning to rename it Fort Schuyler. When Ganesvoort refused to surrender the fort, St. Leger had his men surround it.

### Arnold's Rescue of Fort Stanwix

East of Fort Stanwix, Militia General Nicholas Herkimer organized a force of about 800 militiamen to march to the relief of the fort. Scouts reported the

BENEDICT ARNOLD: THE TRAITOR WITHIN

march to St. Leger, and he sent Brant's Indians to set up an ambush. Herkimer's men marched into the ambush near Oriskany, suffering heavy losses, including a wound to Herkimer that was to prove fatal. Bleeding heavily, Herkimer had himself propped up under a tree, sitting on his saddle, puffing his pipe, and directing a counter attack. He had lost more than 150 men, plus another 50 taken prisoner, most of whom would be tortured and scalped. He ordered the survivors back to Fort Dayton, where he died a few days later.

When General Schuyler, at Saratoga, learned about the battle of Oriskany, he realized that if Fort Stanwix now surrendered, St. Leger would have an open path to Albany. That would force Schuyler's outnumbered men to fight both Burgoyne from the north and St. Leger, from the west.

Against the advice of his officers, Schuyler sent a force of 900 Continentals to aid the fort and Arnold agreed to lead them. Outnumbered two to one by St. Leger's army, Arnold was reluctant to try a direct attack, so he decided to try a ruse. He had a prisoner, a Loyalist named Hon Yost Schuyler, who had been sentenced to die for anti-patriotic activities. When his family appealed for his life, Arnold offered him his freedom if he would give false information to the Indians serving under St. Leger.

The plan sounded quixotic, but there were several reasons it could work. Hon Yost was considered "simple-minded," but he was clever enough to understand what Arnold wanted. The Indians knew him and were familiar with spells in which he "spoke in tongues"—a kind of gibberish that convinced them that he could communicate with the Great Spirit and therefore could not lie.

Hon Yost became enthusiastic about the scheme. He practiced saying in the Iroquois language that the greatly feared General Arnold was coming at the head of a huge army. He even shot holes in his coat to make it appear that he had barely escaped Arnold's guards. He also took several Oneidas with him to support his story. In addition, as extra insurance, Arnold kept Hon Yost's brother as a hostage in case of a betrayal.

Arnold's ruse was wildly successful. The Indians quickly packed up. They had been disappointed in St. Leger and in the heavy losses they had suffered in the ambush at Oriskany. When St. Leger tried to persuade them not to leave, "they grew furious," he wrote, "seized upon the officers' liquor and clothes, and became more formidable than the enemy. . . ." 4. Abandoned by the Indians, who made up half his army, St. Leger had no choice but to raise the siege and head back to Lake Oswego and the boats that would take him back to Canada.

Arnold left two militia regiments to support the fort and headed back to the Hudson. Once again, Arnold had displayed his extraordinary talents. By saving Fort Stanwix, his actions enabled the Americans to avoid fighting on two fronts.

## The Murder of Jane McCrea

During July and August, Burgoyne's Indian allies caused him increasing grief and trouble by launching a campaign of murder, scalping, and plunder. The climax came when two warriors came into camp waving a fresh scalp of long blond hair. The scalp was quickly recognized as that of Jane McCrea, the fiancé of a Loyalist officer, Lieutenant David Jones.

The incident turned into one of the most famous murders in early American history. Over the years, the case became clouded in romance, legend, and myth, and also interpreted in countless stories and paintings. The most popular story—and probably the most factual—was that Lieutenant Jones had paid two warriors to bring her safely from her home to the British camp. A British officer wrote that

> . . . They at first treated her with every mark of civility . . . and were conducting her into camp, when within a mile of it, a dispute arose between the two [over] whose prisoner she was; and words growing very high, one of them . . . fearful of losing the reward . . . most inhumanely struck his tomahawk into her skull and she instantly expired. 5.

Although Burgoyne had tried to hold the Indians in check, the murder fed a rumor that Burgoyne was paying a bounty for rebel scalps. Stories of the murder spread like wildfire throughout New York and New England. Hundreds of men grabbed their muskets and headed for the Patriot camp.

## The Eve of Battle

On his way back from Fort Stanwix (renamed Fort Schuyler), Arnold received the jolting news that his friend Schuyler was being replaced by General

Horatio Gates, now a favorite of Congress. Schuyler was humiliated and so disappointed he could not manage to talk to anyone for several days. He wrote of "the Indignity of being relieved of the command of the army at a time when an Engagement must soon take place." 6.

Benedict Arnold was also furious with Congress when he learned that his request to have his seniority restored was turned down. He was also displeased that Gates was now his commanding officer. In their first meeting, Gates offered no word of thanks for his role in defeating St. Leger. Later, in his diary, Arnold wrote: "Gates only grunted when I returned victorious. Congress decreed to Herkimer a monument; to Ganesvoort a vote of thanks and a command; to Willet [second in command at Stanwix] public praise and an elegant sword; to me nothing." 7.

Although both Arnold and Schuyler were deeply disappointed, the mood in the American camp had changed completely from the previous doubts and fears. The victories at Bennington and then Fort Stanwix had caused dramatic changes in both armies. Burgoyne had suffered the loss of St. Leger's army as well as heavy casualties at Bennington. He was now cut off from Canada, and in desperate need of supplies. American General John Glover wrote in a letter:

> I think matters look fair on our side and I have not the least doubt of beating or compelling Mr. Burgoyne to turn back at least to Ticonderoga, if not to Canada. His situation is dangerous, which he must see and know if he is not blind, and if he is not strong enough to move down to fight us, he cannot remain where he is without giving us a great advantage. 8.

Even the arrival of Gates added to the growing Patriot confidence, although he had no battle experience and had done little to earn his promotion. However, he was popular in Congress and with the soldiers from New England, men who had not cared much for Schuyler and his aristocratic manner. Finally, the arrival of Morgan and his 330 riflemen was cheered. In addition to their sharp-shooting skills, the Patriots believed the woodsmen would keep the Indians under control.

Everyone knew that a battle was coming, and many expected it to be huge—a do-or-die struggle for both sides. Colonel Alexander Scammell wrote to his brother that Burgoyne's army "is driven to desperation and a most bloody Battle must ensue." 9.

The two-part battle of Saratoga turned out to be the turning point of the American Revolution and is considered one of the most important battles in history. Not surprisingly, Benedict Arnold played a vital part in the conflict.

## The First Battle of Freeman's Farm

The Hudson Valley in the region of Saratoga was a picturesque area of steep, forested bluffs rising 300 feet above the river. The bluffs were separated by ravines with narrow streams winding down to the river.

On one of the bluffs, called Bemis Heights, the Patriots found an ideal place for defense. An engineer named Thaddeus Kosciuozko, a volunteer from Poland who had joined the Patriot cause, planned a strong defensive network of three-sided breastworks, nearly a mile long, bristling with cannons. This solid fortification was completed by mid-September. The strong defense of Lake Champlain had given the Patriots nearly twelve months to establish the outstanding defense. General Gates was pleased with the defense. He did not believe in going out to meet the enemy and felt comfortable in staying in the fortress-like defenses and waiting for the British to come to him.

At about the time the American defenses were being completed, Burgoyne had a bridge of boats built across the river and his army moved to the west bank of the Hudson. The river below the crossing had rough rapids, making it impossible for supplies to reach Burgoyne by boat. It was now necessary for Burgoyne to rely on much slower wagons.

When Gates's scouts spotted Burgoyne's army crossing the Hudson, the general ordered his commanders to prepare for battle. He had divided his army into two wings. Gates commanded the right wing and he wisely placed Arnold in command on the left. He did not trust Arnold's tendency to rush into battle, so this arrangement allowed him to direct Arnold's actions. New militia troops were coming in every day, encouraged by the victories at Bennington and Fort Stanwix, and in response to the murder of Jane McCrea. By mid-September, the Americans numbered nearly 10,000, while Burgoyne was now limited to less than 7,000.

The morning of September 19 dawned cold and damp, a sharp change from days of blistering heat. A thick fog blanketed the ravines until mid-morning. When Gates informed his officers that they would fight from behind the breastworks, General Arnold was horrified. He knew that, from the river, Burgoyne's artillery could smash holes in the Americans' right wing and follow with a bayonet attack. He argued that allowing the British to gain the initiative would be suicide.

The land in front of the American line was called Freeman's Farm. The farm included a large cleared field, with dense woods beyond. Arnold wanted to move into the woods and, from there, attack Burgoyne's right, forcing them into that clearing. Gates resisted. Other officers supported Arnold's aggressive plan and Gates finally gave in, at least partly. He would allow Arnold to send Morgan's riflemen, backed by Dearborn's light infantry, to move into the woods flanking Freeman's Farm.

Burgoyne ordered his army forward in three columns. Riedesel, commanding most of the Germans, advanced on the left flank along the river. General Simon Fraser was on the right, and Burgoyne commanded the center. Fraser's men found the rugged terrain difficult and by the time they were far enough west to attack, they were more than two miles from the center column. Finally, around two o'clock, all three columns were in position, and cannons were fired to signal the assault on the American lines.

Burgoyne's plan was to catch the Americans by surprise, and it probably would have worked, with Fraser's troops charging down on the American defenses. But Arnold's idea of moving out to meet the enemy meant that it was the British who were surprised. Morgan's riflemen, some climbing high in trees, hit the advancing British hard, picking off the officers with deadly accuracy. As Fraser's men reeled back into the clearing, Morgan's and Dearborn's men charged after them, but were suddenly stopped cold by the center of Burgoyne's line.

The fighting then became general, with the two sides blasting at each other for four hours. The clearing was frequently filled with smoke, as well as the boom of cannons and the rattle of musket fire. By late afternoon, the clearing was littered with the dead and wounded of both sides. No one dared go to the aid of the wounded because the enemy was so close.

Men on both sides were astounded by the sheer magnitude of noise and violence. British Lieutenant William Digby wrote that he had never imagined such an "explosion of fire . . ."

> . . . the heavy artillery, joining in concert like great peals of thunder, assisted by the echoes of the woods, almost deafened us with the noise. . . . The crash of cannon and musketry never ceased till darkness parted us, when they retired to their camp, leaving us masters of the field; but it was a dear bought victory if I can give it that name, as we lost many brave men. 10.

Burgoyne could—and did—claim victory, simply because his troops were still on part of the battlefield, while the Americans went back to their camp. Although the British had lost 600 men (160 dead, 364 wounded, and 42 missing), twice the total of American losses, Burgoyne confidently wrote to his commander of the garrison at Ticonderoga: "We have had a smart and very honorable action, and are now encamped in front of the field, which must demonstrate our victory beyond the power of even an American newspaper to explain away." 11.

There was some dispute over Benedict Arnold's role in the battle. His insistence on carrying the fighting to the British, rather than waiting behind the Bemis Heights defensive works, was certainly crucial in enabling the Americans to fight Burgoyne's army to a standstill. For example, the redcoats' 62$^{nd}$ regiment, which took the brunt of the first attack by Morgan's and Dearborn's regiments, suffered a casualty rate of more than 80 percent.

Did General Arnold lead his men into the battle, or did he remain at headquarters with Gates? The uncertainty about his precise role was created by Colonel James Wilkinson, Gates's adjutant, who insisted, "General Arnold was not out of camp during the whole action." 12.

James Wilkinson was an ambitious young man. In fact, he was so ambitious that he would let nothing stand in the way of his own advancement. He became notorious for changing his loyalties. Wilkinson was with Arnold on his march to Quebec. He became Arnold's aide and stood by him in several difficult situations. Sensing that Arnold was on his way out, he suddenly changed sides and became General Gates's aide, helping to make Gates the "Hero of Saratoga." A few years later, he joined with Aaron Burr in a scheme to create an empire in what is now the American Southwest, but then turned on Burr, who was tried for treason.

A number of men contradicted Wilkinson and provided testimony of Arnold's pivotal role in the action. General Enoch Poor, for example, wrote that "Arnold rushed into the thickest of the fight with his usual recklessness, and at times acted like a madman." 13. Captain Ebenezer Wakefield later wrote that Arnold "inspired by the fury of a demon, led a charge by riding in front of the line, his eyes flashing, pointing with his sword . . . with a voice that rang as clear as a trumpet, called upon the men to follow him, . . . and . . . he hurled them like a tornado on the British line." According to Wakefield, "nothing could exceed the bravery of Arnold on this day. . . . There seemed to shoot out from him a magnetic flame that electrified his men and made heroes of all within his influence. He seemed the very genius of war." 14. Henry Brockholst Livingstone, Arnold's aide, said, "Arnold alone is due the honor of our late victory. [He had become] the life and soul of the troops [enjoying] the confidence and affection of his officers and soldiers. They would, to a person, follow him to conquest or death." 15.

Even General Burgoyne, in explaining the conflict to Parliament, wrote that he had expected "Gates would receive the attack in his [defensive] lines." But, "when Arnold chose to give rather than receive the attack," he disrupted Burgoyne's entire battle plan. 16. However, the failure of Gates to emerge from his defenses enabled Burgoyne's forces to stay on the Freeman's Farm land when darkness ended the fighting. The most serious blunder Gates made was refusing Arnold when he pleaded for reinforcements at a point when Benedict was certain that one final push would rout the British right and center. Instead he ordered Arnold back to headquarters then sent out Learned's brigade with no senior officer to lead them. They lost their way and did not help in the final push.

The fighting spirit and ability of the Americans surprised the British. As one officer wrote: "The courage and obstinacy with which the Americans fought were the astonishment of everyone. [They had shown] they were not the contemptible enemy we had . . . imagined them, incapable of standing a regular engagement." 17.

Thomas Anburey, a British volunteer, wrote that "[Although] the glory of the day remained on our side, I am fearful the real advantages resulting from this hard-fought battle will rest on that of the Americans, our army being so much weakened by this engagement as not to be of sufficient strength to venture forth and improve the victory, which may, in the end, put a stop to our intended expedition; the only apparent benefit gained is that we keep possession of the ground where the engagement began." 18.

Baroness von Riedesel added her thoughts on why the Americans fought so well: "Every man [in the region] is a born soldier and a good marksman. . . .The thought of fighting for their country and for freedom made them braver than ever." 19.`

Both sides knew that the fighting at Freeman's Farm had not ended the battle. Burgoyne knew his best hope, probably the only hope, was to push through to Albany and hope that Clinton would move north to meet him, squeezing Gates's army between them. Until the battle could be resumed, Burgoyne decided to stay where he was, and ordered his field commanders to build a series of redoubts (barricades) and entrenchments a little to the north of Bemis Heights. He also wrote to Clinton urging him to speed his march north.

### Heroism Denied

As the Freeman's Farm battle drew to a close, Gates sent a messenger to order Arnold back to headquarters. The timing could not have been worse. Arnold had just taken control of several brigades—groups who had become separated from their regiments, and was about to launch a final attack when the order came. By the time he was back in camp, Arnold was furious. And that was just the beginning.

Gates had no intention of letting Benedict Arnold receive credit for the outstanding Patriot success in the Freeman's Farm battle. He was keenly aware of the praise Arnold was receiving from the officers and men of the army and militia. Captain Ebenezer Wakefield, for example, wrote that "Arnold was not only the hero of the field . . . but he had won the admiration of the whole army." 20. To make sure that such praise did not reach beyond the camp, Gates wrote his official report of the battle to Congress without mentioning Benedict Arnold.

By this time, Arnold had had enough. He asked to be discharged from Gates's command. Gates issued a pass for Arnold to go to Washington's headquarters. A number of officers urged him not to leave, so he remained in camp, a general with no troops, ignored at strategy meetings, but not wanting to leave on the eve of what promised to be the decisive battle.

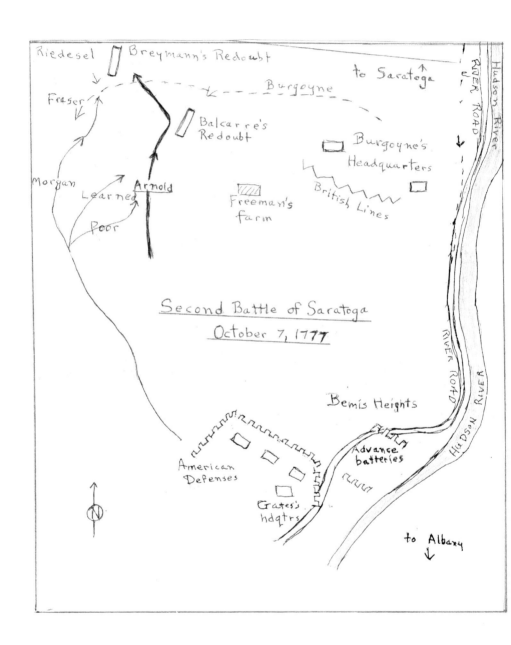

Second Battle of Saratoga
October 7, 1777

# CHAPTER NINE

# The Turning Point, Part II

As thick fog settled over the Saratoga battlefield on the morning of September 20, most of the troops on both sides expected the fighting to resume in a day or two. Instead, an uneasy lull settled over the battle region—a lull that lasted nearly three weeks.

This gap between the two parts of the Battle of Saratoga was hardly a time of rest or inactivity. There were skirmishes every day and night. These were more wearing on the British, since they had no reserves, while new recruits came into the American camp in ever-increasing numbers. In fact, over the course of the eighteen-day lull, Burgoyne's army was becoming steadily weaker, with barely 6,000 men available, while Gates's growing force reached almost 13,000 by the end of September.

The continuing strain on the British was described by Lieutenant Thomas Anburey in his journal:

> . . . The armies are so near that not a night passes but there is firing and continual attacks on the advanced picquets. . . . We are now become so habituated to fire that the soldiers seem to be indifferent to it, and eat and sleep when it is very near them. The officers rest in their cloaths, and the field officers are up frequently in the night.

Anbury also noted a special cause of stress:

> We have, within these few evenings—exclusive of other alarms --been under arms most of the night, as there has been a great noise, like the howling of dogs. . . . The [fourth] night the noise was much greater. [Soldiers were sent to investigate; they discovered the noise] to have arisen from large droves of

wolves that came after the [partially buried] dead bodies. They were similar to a pack of hounds; for one, setting up a cry, they all joined; and when they approached a corpse their noise was hideous till they had scratched it up. 1.

## Burgoyne's Delays and Attrition

Immediately after the battle at Freeman's Farm, General Burgoyne had seemed as confident as ever. He felt certain that General Henry Clinton, now in command in New York City, would approach with the second major part of the invasion plan. The two British armies would then squeeze Gates's army between them, ensuring Burgoyne's greatest triumph.

However, day after day passed with no word from Clinton. Burgoyne sent messages, but never knew that the messengers never got through. They had been caught by Patriots, forced to cough up the bullet-size message capsules, and were then executed as spies.

Finally, late in September, he heard from Clinton. Sir Henry wrote that he would make a push to the north about September 25, "if you think 2,000 men can assist you . . ." 2. Burgoyne was delighted. For some reason he seemed to think the additional 2,000 men, especially if coming from the south, would save the campaign. He decided to stay where he was, strengthen his defenses, and wait for Clinton. His weak right flank, which Arnold and Morgan had attacked on September 19, was now strengthened by the building of two fortifications, called *redoubts*. The largest, the Balcarres Redoubt, was a mound of logs and earth, twelve to fourteen feet high, which stretched for 500 yards. The smaller Breymann Redoubt ran for half that length, with two crude cabins filling the space in between.

Days continued to pass with no more word from Clinton. By October 1st, the mild days gave way to freezing nights. The trees on the hillsides of the Berkshires and Taconics were turning brilliant shades of red, orange, yellow, and green—a grim kind of beauty for the invaders because it meant the onset of a very uncertain winter. Mornings brought frost and touches of snow to the hills, while thick fog filled the river valleys.

In the British and German camps, hungry soldiers now shivered through the nights with empty stomachs. Even with strict rationing, food staples—mostly salt pork and flour—were running dangerously low. The soldiers, along with wives and children, relied on foraging wheat and corn from fields the owners dared not approach because of the fighting. The need for 200 men or more to guard each foraging party added to the soldiers' weariness.

In addition to illness and deaths, the British-Hessian ranks were diminished by desertions and captures. Burgoyne had also lost most of his Indian warriors, originally numbering about 1,000. He had trusted that the rugged, wooded landscape would be ideal for Iroquois-style warfare. Instead, he lamented, "not a man of them was to be brought within the sound of a rifle shot." 3. Barely 100 remained by late September.

Finally, on October 4, Burgoyne knew he dared wait no longer for Clinton. Apparently, as *Saratoga* historian Richard M. Ketchum has pointed out, Burgoyne was not aware that Clinton planned only to make a limited thrust north, because he was unwilling to endanger the major base at New York City. Also, Sir William Howe, the British supreme commander, who was now pressuring Washington near Philadelphia, would not have approved a major campaign. (On October 7, Clinton did make his move: after capturing two Patriot Hudson River forts, he withdrew to New York.)

On the night of October 4th, Burgoyne called his general for a war council. He later wrote of the meeting:

> No intelligence having been received of the expected cooperation . . . it was judged advisable to make a movement to the enemy's left, not only to discover whether there were any possible means of forcing a passage, should it be necessary to advance, or of dislodging him for the convenience of a retreat, but also to cover a forage [mission] of the army, which was in the greatest distress on account of the scarcity. 4.

Burgoyne's generals felt that his plan of sending all but 800 men on the attack was too risky, so he scaled it down to a "reconnaissance in force" of about

2,200. Riedesel, commander of the hired Germans, felt he had to go along with the plan, although he argued it would have been wiser to recross the Hudson, establish themselves closer to Ticonderoga, and there wait for Clinton. Burgoyne, of course, was not at all ready to retreat.

The attack was planned for the morning of October 6th or 7th.

## Showdown at Freeman's Farm

Throughout the long delay between battles, Benedict Arnold remained in the Patriot camp, miserable, humiliated, and alone. His feud with Horatio Gates grew steadily worse, with frequent shouting matches. The arguments were so fierce that one of Arnold's aides worried in a letter to Schuyler, "General Arnold is so much offended at the treatment Gates has given him that I have not the least doubt the latter will be called on [for a duel]." Schuyler answered: "Perhaps [Gates] is so very sure of success that he does not wish Arnold to come in for a share of it." 5.

On the morning of October 7th, scouts reported the beginning of the British advance. Burgoyne again sent General Fraser's force to try to circle the American left, sending even more men than in September, hoping to place artillery to hit the American fortification from one side, while Riedesel's artillery opened up from the Hudson.

For three hours, General Gates did almost nothing, until he finally sent Morgan and Dearborn "to begin the game." The firing did not begin until the afternoon, when a British force opened fire on a group of the Americans, then launched a bayonet attack. The Americans held their ground and fired volleys that forced the redcoats to retreat.

The sound of the gunfire was almost too much for Arnold. He paced back and forth, futilely trying to see the action through binoculars. The gunfire sounds increased as Morgan's riflemen circled the enemy right and forced them to retreat into the woods, while Dearborn's men caught them in a withering crossfire. The advance was finally stopped when Hessian colonel, the Earl of Balcarres, rallied his men behind their redoubt.

Gates had briefly allowed Arnold, accompanied by General Lincoln, to survey the battlefield. When they returned, Arnold insisted that Gates commit a strong force on the left to support Morgan and Dearborn. Gates snapped, "General Arnold, I have nothing for you to do. You have no business here." 6.

Minutes after that rebuke, Arnold leaped on a borrowed horse and galloped to the battlefield. At this point, Benedict Arnold took over the battle. Military historian W. J. Wood wrote of Arnold's critical role: "Gates was not there, nor did he ever show himself outside his headquarters. Benedict Arnold *was* there, and that fact turned the next phase of Bemis Heights into a decisive battle." 7.

Arnold came up to Learned's brigade, being held in reserve along with several regiments of Connecticut militia. When told where the militia were from, he shouted: "My old Norwich and New London friends! God bless you!" The men cheered as he spurred his horse forward. "Now come on, boys, if the day is long enough, we'll have them in hell before night." 8.

Learned willingly let Arnold take command, and he led a charge against the Balcarres Redoubt. Under heavy fire, the Americans had almost pushed their way through the tangled logs and sharpened sticks, but the British and Hessian resistance was so fierce that Arnold ordered a withdrawal.

He made a quick survey of the battlefield and realized he had attacked the strongest of the redoubts. He wheeled his horse to the left and made a wild gallop between the two armies, with bullets flying in both directions. A Connecticut militiaman wrote: "He behaved, as I then thought, more like a madman than a cool and discreet officer." 9. But British historian Sir John Fortescue saw it differently: "With true military instinct," he wrote, "Arnold seized the opportunity to order a general attack upon the British entrenchments." 10. Meantime, Gates, learning that Arnold had left the camp, sent Major John Armstrong to bring him back, but Armstrong wisely stayed out of the way.

There was no stopping Benedict Arnold now. Sweeping up parts of different regiments, the attack gained strength, with Arnold out in front on horseback, waving his sword, and shouting encouragement to the men. The British and Germans were soon in a chaotic, every-man-for-himself retreat. Either Ar-

nold or Morgan noticed that British General Simon Fraser, mounted on a big
gray horse was rallying large numbers to make a stand, and one of them ordered
a marksman to bring him down from a great distance, which he did with his
third shot. Hit in the stomach, Fraser slumped over his saddle as two aides led
him away. (He died the next day.) Burgoyne, seeing his friend and most important general hit, seemed to lose heart; he may also have realized that he was not
going to win this critical struggle, and he ordered his men to withdraw into
their battlements.

General Arnold could have been satisfied with driving the enemy from the
field, but as long as the two redoubts remained and Burgoyne could come back
again, he had no intention of stopping. In a hastily created plan with Morgan,
Arnold would circle around the rear of Breymann's Redoubt, while Morgan
and Dearborn attacked from the front. The double assault took the defenders
by surprise. Colonel Breymann tried to rally his men, shouting and threatening
to kill anyone who fled, but he was shot, possibly by one of his own men, and
the defense began to crumble.

As Arnold led one charge through gunfire and clouds of smoke into the redoubt, Morgan's men attacked from the front. The Hessians, plus some British
and Canadians, were now in full, frantic flight. A few of the Hessians stopped
to fire one last volley. One of the musket balls slammed into Arnold's leg—
the same leg that had been seriously wounded in Quebec. Several bullets hit
his horse, and the animal crashed to the ground, landing heavily on Arnold's
stricken leg, causing several compound fractures.

Arnold continued to shout encouragement to "my brave boys," as Morgan's
men poured into the redoubt, forcing the few remaining British and Hessians
to surrender. Morgan's and Dearborn's men rushed to pull Arnold from under
his horse. One of the men was about to bayonet the Hessian youth whose shot
had felled Arnold. The stricken general shouted not to kill him; he was only
doing his duty.

Patriot soldiers made a makeshift litter out of blankets and carried Arnold
to Gates's headquarters. With no doctor on the battlefield, Benedict must have
been in unbelievable pain, but he remained conscious long enough to accept the

praise and congratulations of many of the officers and men. Horatio Gates said nothing to him, and apparently never wrote to ask about his recovery. Arnold was placed on a cart for a bouncing, 30-mile ride to the Continental Army Hospital in Albany. Although his survival was uncertain, he adamantly refused to let doctors amputate the bloody leg with half a dozen bones jutting through the skin.

Darkness was settling over the battlefield as Arnold was carted off. Over the next twenty-four hours, the impact of his leadership on the battle was suggested by the losses on both sides. The British lost 184 killed, 264 wounded, and 183 captured—a total of 631, including 31 officers. And the Germans had 94 killed, 67 wounded, and 102 taken prisoner. Burgoyne's total losses, then, were 894, nearly half of his attacking force. The American losses were remarkably light: an estimated 30 killed and 100 wounded.

## Retreat and Surrender

The next morning, Burgoyne's battered army remained behind strong defensive works, facing an ever-growing army of militia as well as the Continentals who had borne the brunt of the fighting. By mid-October, General Gates had more than 16,000 troops at his command. Burgoyne's retreat and the final decision to surrender involved delays and indecision. He seemed to cling to the hope that Clinton might still come to his rescue.

Finally, on the night of the 8th, the army began its slow, painful retreat north. Through the night and the next day, they had advanced only eight miles. A wind-driven rain made the march even more miserable. Gates, nearly as slow to move as Burgoyne, managed to send several militia units to race up the east side of the Hudson to take positions north of the British, cutting off their retreat beyond the village of Saratoga. Morgan's riflemen and other units advanced to the west of the British, completing the net that encircled Burgoyne.

After several days more, the British reached Saratoga, where they torched General Schuyler's estate, and tried to set up a defensive perimeter. Baron von Riedesel describes their condition:

> . . . the ground was covered with dead horses that had either
> been killed by the enemy's bullets or by exhaustion, as there

had been no forage for several days. . . . Even for the wounded, no spot could be found which could afford them a safe shelter—not even . . . long [enough] for a surgeon to bind up their ghastly wounds. The whole camp was now a scene of constant fighting. . . . The sick and wounded would drag themselves along into a quiet corner of the woods and lie down to die on the damp ground. . . . 11.

Even in the midst of the suffering and bloodshed, there were incidents of remarkable kindness extended to an enemy. The case of British Major John Dyke Acland and Lady Acland provides a good example. The major, wounded in both legs, was captured and taken to the army hospital in Albany. His distraught young wife traveled with Baroness von Riedesel on the retreat, until the baroness finally persuaded her to seek a pass to American lines in the hope of joining her husband. Burgoyne wrote the pass and Lady Acland, accompanied by a minister and two others, that night boarded an open boat for a rain-drenched journey down the Hudson to American lines.

With a drum beating a parley, the boat was allowed to land its passengers. Major Dearborn, who was in command of the American line, invited the very wet and quite pregnant ladyship to his house for a cup of tea and a night's rest before a blazing fire. In the morning, General Gates had her escorted to her husband in Albany. Gates, in a letter to his wife, called her ladyship "the most amiable, delicate piece of Quality you ever beheld." 12. (After the major's eleven-week recovery, the couple traveled to British headquarters in New York City.)

On October 13, Burgoyne held a "solemn council of war," at which his generals agreed that surrender was now their only option. After three days of negotiations, surrender ceremonies were held on October 17th at Saratoga between Burgoyne, resplendent in his carefully-preserved scarlet uniform and the bespectacled Gates in a plain blue coat, managing to look much like his nickname of "Granny Gates."

The immediate results of Saratoga were staggering. General John Burgoyne's once glittering invasion force of 10,000 trained troops had been knocked out of the war. The ragged remnants of that army, now stacking their weapons at Saratoga, included nine generals, nearly 400 other officers, and more than 5,000 troops of lesser rank.

The long-term results made the battle even more significant as *the* turning point of the American Revolution. The victory finally persuaded France to enter the war as a full-fledged ally of the United States. This meant a vital infusion of weapons, ammunition, and other war material, as well as troops and the powerful French navy. In addition, England now faced the likelihood of a land war in Europe against France and its allies.

The timing of the victory was also crucial. The main Continental Army, led by Washington, had just lost two major battles to the British under Howe at Germantown and Brandywine Creek in Pennsylvania, forcing Congress to flee to the town of York. The two defeats had caused a serious decline in Patriot morale. Within Congress and the army, an underground movement—later known as the Conway cabal—developed with the apparent aim of removing Washington and replacing him with General Gates. Saratoga changed everything.

Still another positive outcome of the battle was that thousands of militiamen learned the value of discipline. They had beaten a professional European army—an enemy that assumed Americans would run away when confronted by trained British redcoats. Instead the militia volunteers learned to listen to their officers and to observe the Continentals, with the result that they stood fast, even in the face of a bayonet charge.

As the British and Germans marched between rows of Americans to stack their weapons, they were relieved and gratified to find that "not a single man gave any evidence or the slightest impression of feeling hatred, mockery, or malicious pleasure or pride for our miserable fate; [instead] it seemed rather as though they desired to do us honor." Lord Francis Napier added: "They behaved with the greatest decency and propriety, not even a smile appearing in any of their countenances. . . ." 13.

Benedict Arnold, of course, was not present for the British retreat or the surrender ceremonies. He received frequent reports from visitors and asked countless questions. What troubled him most, in addition to his shattered leg and uncertain future, was that Gates was there to accept Burgoyne's sword and receive credit for the victory. Several years later Arnold wrote in his diary:

> . . . I effaced myself and saved America. For Saratoga will be placed by future historians among the fifteen decisive battles of the world. It was the Blenheim of the Revolution; and the future historian shall say, 'One General won it; and that was not the General in command.' 14.

At the time of the surrender, Arnold was not yet aware of how much harm Horatio Gates could do him, aided by his equally ambitious assistant, James Wilkinson.

## The Rise and Fall of Horatio Gates

Following the surrender at Saratoga, members of Congress could not find enough ways to pile praise and honors on General Gates. They voted to have a special gold medal struck to honor his leadership, the first such medal since the gold piece commemorating General Washington for forcing the British to evacuate Boston in 1776.

No one in Congress seemed troubled by Gates's failure to make more than the briefest mention of Benedict Arnold, or that he sent no report to Washington, the commander-in-chief. Instead, Gates heaped praise on Wilkinson, calling him a "military genius." He urged Congress to reward his aide. This was done and Wilkinson emerged as a brevet brigadier; his elevation to general status shocked and dismayed the army's generals. Some wondered if serving in the Continental Army was worth the personal sacrifices, when men like Wilkinson could be promoted without any sacrifices.

Wilkinson did his best to promote his own cause. He pigeon-holed members of Congress, especially those who supported Gates. In letters to friends, he insisted that "Benedict Arnold neither rendered service nor deserved credit" for Saratoga. 15.

The Congressional approval of General Gates became less certain when terms of the surrender were studied. Gates had granted Burgoyne almost everything he asked for. He even agreed to call the treaty a "convention" rather than a "capitulation." The British and Germans were to be marched to Boston, where they would board transport ships to England, where they agreed not to return to the war.

A majority in Congress, as well as Washington, agreed that the terms were far too lenient. Early in 1778, Congress used technicalities to change those conditions. While Burgoyne and his aides were allowed to return to England, the rest of the defeated army was marched to the interior of Virginia for the remainder of the war. Gates was not criticized for his negotiations. As Henry Laurens said in announcing the gold medal: "Your name, Sir, will be written in the breasts of the grateful Americans of the present age and sent down to posterity in characters which will remain indelible when the gold [of the medal] shall have changed in appearance." 16.

In spite of his few mistakes and his lack of real involvement in the battle, Horatio Gates was to go down in history as "The Hero of Saratoga."

General Gates enjoyed his status as hero until the summer of 1780. With the American forces in the South in some disarray, Congress decided to send Gates to create stability. Washington was not consulted, probably because he would not have approved.

Against the advice of his officers, Gates launched his half-trained militia against a British force at Camden, South Carolina in the pre-dawn hours of August 16, 1780. The Battle of Camden quickly became a bloody defeat for the Americans. Gates fled the battlefield and by nightfall was in North Carolina, more than sixty miles north of Camden.

An embarrassed Congress immediately recalled Gates, and this time asked Washington to name a successor. The commander-in-chief named General Nathanael Greene to command the Southern Department; Greene proceeded to conduct a brilliant duel with the British under Cornwallis that led to the final battle at Yorktown. Although Gates remained the second-ranking general, the luster was off his status as hero. Disenchanted Congressmen ignored Gates's request for a court of inquiry to clear his name.

Gates's critics had a grand time with the Camden fiasco, especially when Gates rode another 120 miles north in just two days. Alexander Hamilton wrote: "Was there ever such an instance of a general running away . . . from his whole army? And was there ever so precipitous a flight? . . . It does admirable credit to the activity of a man at his time of life." 17. And a Loyalist newspaper in New York ran a long advertisement by "Horatio Gates" seeking information about a lost or missing army.

The Gates embarrassment came too late to help Benedict Arnold. A month after the Battle of Camden, Arnold's reputation was destroyed by the exposure of his far greater betrayal.

### Benedict Arnold's Turning Point?

When Arnold was carried off the battlefield at the conclusion of his heroism at Freeman's Farm, Major Dearborn bent down to him and asked where he had been hit. According to Dearborn, Arnold answered that it was the same leg and wished "the ball had passed his heart." 18.

Had the shot killed him, he might have died as the martyred hero of Saratoga. It would have made it much harder for Gates and Wilkinson to eclipse his role. And he would have gained the fame he craved as one of the great battlefield leaders in America's history.

Instead, Benedict faced a bleak future in the army's hospital in Albany. Day after day he lay in agonizing pain, while doctors insisted that the leg had to come off to avoid gangrene. He repeatedly resisted their "damned nonsense," even though pieces of bone were jutting through his mangled flesh. In an effort to straighten the leg and stabilize it, the doctors constructed a "fracture box"— a sort of wooden cast that forced Arnold to lie on his back, virtually motionless, a maddening confinement, especially for a man of action.

Arnold's condition remained unchanged through October, November, and December. Finally, in January, 1778, he felt well enough to sit up, but the movement burst open the wound, and he fell back on the bed as searing pain shot through his leg and body. Several more weeks passed before he succeeded in sitting up. From that point through the spring the leg healed quickly, although he would remain disabled for life. The long confinement had caused the muscles to atrophy, and the injured leg emerged two inches shorter.

During these weeks of agony, Arnold had little to do but to think, and to reflect on how Gates and Wilkinson had stolen from him the fruits of victory. Throughout his military career, he had hurled himself into one military crisis after another. He had been the ideal field commander—absolutely fearless and determined, with a unique ability to see the pitfalls and possibilities in every situation; he was a constant source of inspiration to his men, while also showing a deep concern for their well-being. Henry Brockholst Livingstone, who served as Arnold's aide during the Saratoga campaign, wrote that "Arnold alone is due the honor of our late victory; [he had become] the life and soul of his troops, [enjoying] the confidence and affection of his officers and soldiers. They would, to a person, follow him to conquest or death." 19.

Arnold had been certain that these heroic efforts would help to restore his family name, honor, and fortune. Instead, he spent the discouraging months of convalescence wondering how everything could have gone so wrong.

The authors of two recent studies offered the following assessments of Benedict Arnold at this stage:

> Richard M. Ketchum, *Saratoga, Turning Point of the American Revolution* (1997): "Benedict Arnold was now thirty-six years old, a major general, and the kind of field commander generals dream about—fearless and daring, a natural leader, with stamina and determination that allowed nothing to stand in his way. . . .
>
> On the strength of his record there was no question about Arnold's remarkable ability as a battlefield leader, but behind the record and beneath the surface was a man driven by terrible self-doubts and a hunger for fame, social acceptance, money, and rank that had thus far, been denied him. He was a man whose pride was easily wounded, one who could accept neither opposition to his ideas nor criticism while at the same time being totally insensitive to the feelings of others." 20.
>
> James Kirby Martin, *Benedict Arnold* (1997): "As the New

Year dawned, deep and bitter resentment was infusing Arnold's troubled soul. As he grappled with the prospect of life as a virtual cripple, he kept asking himself what it had all been for, why the personal sacrifice when his only reward was defamed personal honor. With time passing so slowly, Arnold kept searching for reasonable answers to his question, but he could not find them." 21.

But was there more? Was the disappointment and resentment enough to explain his decision to betray the cause he had fought and bled for? He wanted fame for his military leadership; he also wanted to restore his family name and his fortune. Could turning traitor bring him closer to any of those goals?

Early 1778 may be too soon to draw conclusions about why Arnold became America's most notorious traitor. For more conclusive evidence we need to explore further the twisted, tortured path of the next three years.

The co-conspirators—John Andre., Peggy Shippen Arnold,
and Benedict Arnold

Arnold's men struggling against the flooded Dead River.

American and British ships exchange fire at Valcour Island, Oct. 11, 1776.

Arnold receiving a life-threatening wound at the second Battle of Saratoga.

# Chapter Ten

## Twists And Turns

The first six months of 1778 were times of great uncertainty for Arnold, with many unexpected twists and turns. The year began with his slow-and-only-partial recovery from his wound. In mid-January, about the time of his abortive attempt to sit up, he received a letter from Washington.

### Mis-Communication With Washington

The commander apologized for not contacting him sooner (but did not take the time to explain how he had been struggling against the internal enemies who were trying to replace him with Horatio Gates). Washington asked "whether you are upon your legs again, and if you are not, may I flatter myself that you will be soon? . . . No one wishes more sincerely for this event than I do." He ended the letter by stating "the earnest wish to have your services [in] the ensuing campaign; [Washington promised] . . . a command which I trust will be agreeable to yourself and of great advantage to the public." 1.

Arnold was slow to respond to his commander's warm words. Washington had no way of knowing that his fighting general was battling pain and depression from the re-opening of his wound. He was also furious about the ways he had been humiliated by General Gates and by Congress, and also by the outlandish praise Congress had heaped on Gates.

Six weeks passed before Arnold finally answered Washington, on March 12, from Middletown, Connecticut, where he had been staying with friends. He also apologized for taking so much time to reply, blaming his wounds for the delay. The wounds, he explained, had been "closed" but had recently "broke out again, occasioned by some loose splinters of bone remaining in the leg, which will not be serviceable until they are extracted. . . . It will take time, perhaps two, and possibly five or six months." 2. He could not say when he would be able to travel to headquarters "and take the command your Excellency has been so good as to reserve for me."

Washington wrote again in early May to describe a gift he wished to give Arnold. The gift had come from France—three sets of epaulets and sword knots. The commander was to keep one set and to use the other two to honor special individuals. He wrote that he wished to present one set to Arnold, "as a testimony of my sincere regard and approbation of your conduct." 3.

General Washington was not a demonstrative person and had difficulty expressing his feelings, especially to men, so this gift of decorative epaulets and sword knots probably represented as much warmth as he could manage. To Arnold, however, with his feelings of betrayal by the cause for which he had given so much, the gift may have seemed a hollow gesture. Arnold barely mentioned it in his memoirs. The gift and the reaction show how little the two men understood each other. Washington clearly had little idea of the bitterness and disappointment that was poisoning Arnold's soul.

Two weeks later, with no advance notice, a carriage pulled up at Washington's headquarters at Valley Forge, and Benedict Arnold painfully stepped out, leaning heavily on a crutch. From Washington's point of view, Arnold probably appeared to be a dedicated Patriot, determined to be ready for the next campaign. Although the commander must have been startled by the severity of Arnold's disability, he could still hope that Benedict would again be his fighting general.

## Military Governor of Philadelphia

Convinced that General Arnold was not yet able to take a field command, Washington offered him another post: The British were about to evacuate Philadelphia and General Howe was returning to New York. As soon as the British left in June, 1778, Benedict Arnold would become military governor of the city. Washington's appointment was understandable. Since his favorite general could hardly stand, much less sit a horse or give orders in the field, a few months at a governor's desk seemed like a good solution until he was more fully recovered.

The commander had rarely made a more ill-advised appointment; it thrust

Arnold into a maelstrom of political conflict and intrigue that he was not equipped to handle. Congress was moving back to Philadelphia from York, so old conflicts would inevitably be renewed, and delegates could watch him closely for any mistakes. In addition, a new state government had been formed and its leader, Joseph Reed, was determined to protect the state's independent powers in the face of any encroachments by Congress, or interference by Military Governor Benedict Arnold.

In addition, the situation would reveal some of Benedict's most serious flaws. Knowing that he was famous only as a battlefield leader, he became determined to show that he came from a famous family and was the equal of the very best in Philadelphia society. He also had decided that he would now look after his own interests, since his many sacrifices for the Revolution had gained him little. He seemed to want all that had been denied him—wealth, honors, and respect. In the months ahead, his desires were seen by many as signs of greed, aggressiveness, and arrogance.

In spite of his weaknesses, which his enemies attacked frequently, the better side of his nature sometimes emerged. He could be gracious in society and, more important, he displayed kindness and compassion toward those in need.

Here are some of the highlights of his career as military governor:

As soon as the British evacuated Philadelphia in June, 1778, Military Governor Benedict Arnold quickly established his new lifestyle. He leased one of the finest mansions in the city—the one that the British commander General Howe had occupied. He dressed in splendid new uniforms and purchased the finest furnishings for the house. He employed a housekeeper, a cook, a coachman, and a groom, as well as seven lesser servants. His sister Hannah and his three sons moved to Philadelphia, and the family rode about the city in a handsome carriage, served by a team of four and liveried attendants. Governor Arnold also became known for elegant dinners, to which he invited leading citizens, including many who had remained neutral or cooperated with the British during the occupation.

Arnold used his own money for most of these expenses. When Hannah detailed how high the bills were running, he blamed Congress for much of the financial tangle, in part because he had received no pay for more than three years of military service, nor had he been reimbursed for the many expenses and losses he had encountered. In one of his many criticisms of Congress, he wrote: "It is a matter much to be lamented that our army is permitted to starve in a land of plenty; [those responsible] should be capitally punished." 4.

In the summer of 1778, he found a way to help the orphaned children of Dr. Joseph Warren, one of the first heroes of the Revolution, who had been killed at Bunker Hill. Warren had been instrumental in sending Arnold to Ticonderoga in 1775. He wrote to Miss Mercy Scollay, who had been engaged to be the doctor's second wife and was now caring for his son and daughter. Since Massachusetts had done nothing to assist them, Arnold wrote that he was sending five hundred dollars to help. This was not simply a matter of sending money. He added, "I wish to have Richard clothed handsomely, and sent to the best school in Boston. [For] any expense you are at, please call on me . . . and it will be paid with thanks." 5.

Two months later, he sent Mercy another five hundred dollars and promised to keep after Congress to help. He kept his promise and repeatedly agitated for Congress to step in. The delegates finally did act and provided funds for the families of deceased officers. Mercy Scollay received this pronouncement a few weeks after Arnold's treason was exposed.

Joseph Reed of the Council of Pennsylvania was to prove the most dangerous of all of Arnold's enemies. Reed had taken a dislike to Arnold as soon as they met in 1778, and he was determined to oppose the military governor whenever he could. The ardent Patriots in the state's government were eager to punish Philadelphia's Loyalists for aiding the British or cooperating with them, during the British occupation.

Reed had a long list of Loyalists, including many Quakers, whom he wanted tried and, if found guilty, executed. The execution of two Quakers had already taken place before Arnold took office. The new military governor first collided with the state leader when Arnold decreed an end to all executions. He had the vigorous support of Washington, who wanted him to pursue a policy of reconciliation.

The state's Patriot leaders wanted not only to get rid of Loyalists, but also

to seize their property as well. When Reed acquired the house of Joseph Galloway, a well-known Loyalist, he again crossed swords with Arnold. Reed had the
state militia evict Galloway's wife Grace. When she refused to leave, they carried her out in a chair. Benedict was outraged. He could not stop the eviction,
but he sent his housekeeper to assist her and gave her the use of his carriage.

Arnold also antagonized the Pennsylvania Patriots by pursuing private
business interests. He purchased a schooner and outfitted it as a privateer. He
also learned of a warehouse in New Jersey that was filled with merchandise,
including wine, medical supplies, and civilian clothing. Arnold used government wagons to haul the merchandise to Philadelphia, where it was sold and
the profits split between Arnold and two partners.

Arnold felt justified in pursuing these ventures because he was responsible for
entertaining important visitors from foreign countries, from Congress, and from
the army, and these responsibilities created the need for a well-staffed household.
The practice of using one's position for personal gain was not illegal, and many
others had engaged in it, including leading Patriots. But many people considered
the practice tawdry and unsavory. Washington had referred to a "dirty, mercenary
spirit" creeping into the Revolution. Nevertheless when Joseph Reed reported
Benedict Arnold's dealings to the commander-in-chief, Washington did nothing.

Reed and his Pennsylvania Council stepped up their criticism of Benedict
Arnold, often in newspaper articles. One letter to a pro-Reed newspaper declared, "When I meet your carriage in the streets, and think of the splendor in
which you live and revel . . . it is impossible to avoid the question, 'From whence
have these riches flowed if you did not plunder Montreal.'" 6.

Anti-Arnold forces brought up all the old, unproven charges against him.
Arnold responded to many of the charges, but that seemed only to encourage
more attacks. He was fortunate that 1778, after a slow beginning, also brought
signs of a better life for the troubled general.

## Lonely Months

During his long convalescence at the army hospital in Albany, Benedict was
confined to bed and the fracture box for four painful and lonely months. Spend-

ing day after day in this situation must have made him desperate for human companionship, especially the warmth and physical closeness of a woman. He had been devastated by the death of his wife, and had had no meaningful relationship since. This loneliness might not have mattered much on the battlefield or during the worst weeks of pain and fogginess induced by laudanum or small amounts of opium mixed with alcohol—a common painkilling dependency.

By late January 1778, however, he became well enough to feel the loneliness of his life. During the early spring, Benedict made a spirited bid to re-open his courtship with Elizabeth De Blois. He wrote long, passionate letters to her in Boston, and again enlisted the aid of Lucy Knox. Miss De Blois was somewhat kinder to him this time, even congratulating him on his military achievements, but insisted that they stop the correspondence. He wrote one more time, and receiving no response, had to admit that the matter was closed.

He soon received his appointment as military governor, and became so busy that he had no time to be crushed by the rejection. In fact, only days after his arrival in Philadelphia, he met Margaret "Peggy" Shippen, and a new courtship began.

## Love and Marriage

One of the Loyalist families Benedict met on his arrival in Philadelphia was the Shippens—a wealthy merchant family with three lovely, lively, and intelligent daughters. The youngest—Peggy—was just turning eighteen that month of June. She was widely regarded as the most beautiful and accomplished belle of Philadelphia. She could use her prettiness to have young men constantly fawning over her; as one British naval officer wrote, "We were all in love with her." 7. Peggy quickly captured Benedict's attention. In fact, in very little time, he was hopelessly in love.

By all accounts, Peggy Shippen was a remarkable young woman. After examining contemporary accounts of her, historian Willard Sterne Randall described her as " . . . tiny, blond, dainty of face and figure, with steady, wide-set blue-gray eyes. . . . Appearing to be shy, she was bright and quick and capable of conversing at length about politics and business to anyone." 8.

During the previous year, when the British occupied Philadelphia, Peggy, her two sisters and their friends were invited to concerts, plays, and parties by young British officers almost every evening. Peggy was often in the company of Captain John Andre, a good-looking actor, playwright and poet, as well as the aide-de-camp to General Henry Clinton, who was soon to replace Howe as supreme commander of British forces in America.

Benedict began an intense but controlled courtship (no trunks full of gowns). His efforts must have seemed awkward at first. He was twenty years older and still could not walk, or even stand, without difficulty and pain. The British were gone, but a swarm of agile young men, including Continental soldiers, was now buzzing around her.

Although Arnold's courtship looked like an uphill struggle, he had several things in his favor. First, he was a great military hero, who cut a dashing figure in his major general's uniform. Even his war wound was regarded as a badge of his heroism. He had rather swarthy good looks, with strangely powerful gray eyes. Historian John Richard Allen compiled a composite description based on contemporary accounts: "He was well formed, muscular, capable of great endurance, active, graceful in his movements and exceptionally adept at athletic exercise." 9.

People often spoke of Benedict as arrogant and crude, but he also possessed remarkable charm and eloquence. The best description of this aspect of his personality was a statement by Charles Carroll of Maryland, one of three commissioners sent by Congress to Canada in 1776 (with Benjamin Franklin and Samuel Chase) to find out what was going wrong with the invasion of Quebec. Carroll was greatly impressed by Arnold. He wrote: "An officer bred up at Versailles could not have behaved with more delicate ease and good breeding. . . . If this war continues and Arnold should not be taken off pretty early, he will turn out a great man. He has great vivacity, perseverance, resources, integrity and a cool judgment." 10.

During the summer of 1778, Benedict became a regular at the Shippen home for afternoon tea or dinner. He often escorted Peggy and her sisters to social functions. The Shippens were polite to Arnold, but they were also very uneasy about the idea of having their youngest daughter courted by the most notorious rebel leader. But the couple was also aware that the general was doing more than anyone to protect their freedom and their property. While Peggy's father, Edward Shippen, was not opposed to the courtship, he had not given his approval because he hoped the marriage could be put off until the spring of 1779. He was uneasy about the state of Arnold's finances. He quite likely advised his daughter to be cautious.

The courtship proceeded in a slow and stately manner through the summer, autumn, and winter. He was with Peggy almost daily, and even though the couple was chaperoned by her parents in the Shippen home, they seemed to have ample time alone together.

On September 25, Benedict wrote his proposal letter to Peggy. The letter was romantic and passionate, but also remarkably unusual—unusual because large portions of it were copied word for word from his proposal to Betsy De Blois. Perhaps he felt that his letter to Betsy had achieved an eloquence he could not hope to duplicate. Whatever the case, here are key parts of the letter:

> Twenty times have I taken up my pen to write to you, and as often has my trembling hand refused to obey the dictates of my heart—a heart which, though calm and serene amidst the clashing of arms and all the din and horrors of war, trembles with diffidence and fear of giving offence when it attempts to address you on a subject so important to its happiness. Dear madam, your charms have lighted up a flame in my bosom which can never be extinguished, your heavenly image is too deeply impressed ever to be effaced. . . . On you alone my happiness depends.

As he had done with Betsy, he urged Peggy to suffer

> your heavenly bosom . . . to expand with a sensation more soft, more tender than friendship. . . . Whatever my fate may be, my most ardent wish is for your happiness, and my latest breath will be to implore the blessing of heaven on the idol and only wish of my heart. 11.

Benedict's ardor failed to persuade Peggy to give her consent, and this must have been very difficult for him. After months of enforced celibacy, he had to suppress his desires and behave as an eighteenth century courtier. Toward the close of 1778, family members and friends began to wonder about the long delay. One relative wrote: "Pray tell me, will Cousin Peggy follow your example? Everyone tells me so with such confidence that I am laughed at for my unbelief. Does she know her own mind yet?" Another cousin expressed her surprise in a late January 1779 letter: "… When is he likely to convert our little Peggy? They say she intends to surrender soon. I thought the fort would not hold out so long. Well after all there is nothing like perseverance, and a regular attack." 12.

Peggy finally gave in, and the wedding took place in the Shippen mansion on April 8, 1779. During the marriage ceremony, Arnold had to be supported by a soldier. His pride was probably hurt further during the reception by having his leg propped on a camp stool. But he had also achieved his greatest victory— he had finally won Peggy Shippen's hand.

This happiest of occasions, however, could not spare him from the determined antagonism of his adversaries.

### Intrigue and the First Steps to Treason

In February 1779, Arnold left Philadelphia to meet with Schuyler and others in Albany to finalize New York's property gift—a gift of property and land as a reward for his heroic services. But before he had gone many miles, Joseph Reed stepped in. As soon as he heard about New York's planned gift to Arnold, Reed and his Pennsylvania Council filed formal charges against Arnold, accusing him of eight crimes involving misuse of his office, the charges to be tried in state court. Reed later added that, as long as Arnold remained in office, the state would no longer call out the militia to fight the British, nor would they pay to support the Continental Army.

The timing of Reed's rash action could not have been worse. Arnold was already on his way north when an aide caught up with him and delivered the news. Arnold was crushed. He didn't know what to do—to continue on to New York, or go back to Philadelphia to face the charges.

He did neither. Instead, he went to Washington's headquarters in Morristown and met with the general. Washington, too, was furious and convinced Arnold to ask for a Congressional hearing. Congress referred the charges to a committee, which quickly cleared him of the first six charges for lack of evidence. The two remaining charges involved the use of military wagons, so they would be heard by a military court.

Arnold's problems with Reed and his committee had now expanded into a conflict between Congress and a state. The threat of withholding militia from the Patriot forces could endanger the hope of defeating the British. Members of Congress and the Pennsylvania Council, after an all-night debate, reached a compromise. A new committee was formed, which ordered a new trial for Arnold—on the same eight charges.

Benedict could not believe what was happening to him. Another trial meant more long hours spent gathering all his evidence again. Matters were made worse when he wrote Washington, asking that the trial take place quickly. Washington had originally scheduled a hearing on the two military questions to take place on May 1, but Reed now asked for an indefinite delay, most likely because he still had no evidence.

Once again, Arnold was shocked when Washington agreed to the postponement. It seemed that not only had Congress turned its back on him, but so had Washington, the one man on whom he had always depended. Desperate for support, Arnold wrote an anguished letter to the commander:

> If your Excellency thinks me criminal, for Heaven's sake, let me be immediately tried and, if found guilty, executed. I want no favor; I ask only justice. . . . Having made every sacrifice of fortune and blood, and become a cripple in the service of my country, I little expected to meet the ungrateful returns I have received from my countrymen. But as Congress have stamped ingratitude as the current coin. I must take it. . . .
>
> I have nothing left but the little reputation I had gained in the army. Delay in the present case is worse than death. 14.

Arnold had also expressed his despair in a letter to Peggy shortly before they were married. "I am heartily tired with my journey," he wrote, "and almost so with human nature. I daily discover so much baseness and ingratitude among mankind that I almost blush at being of the same species." 15.

Even the Loyalist *Royal Gazette* commented on the shabby treatment Arnold was receiving: The newspaper first praised him as "more distinguished for valour and perseverance [than any other American commander]. General Arnold heretofore has been styled another Hannibal, but losing a leg in the service of Congress, the latter considering him unfit for any further exercise of his military talents, permit him thus to fall into the unmerciful fangs of the executive council of Pennsylvania." 16.

Arnold's fight to clear his name was to continue through 1779 and into 1780. He never made the trip to New York State to try to finalize the property gift. Why didn't he take advantage of that time to travel north for meetings with Schuyler and others to try to finalize the reward? If successful, the gift would have helped to ease his troubled finances.

Instead, early in May—less than a month after his marriage to Peggy— Benedict made his first contact with the British, the initial step on his zig-zag road to treason. He contacted a Loyalist shopkeeper in Philadelphia named Joseph Stansbury. Arnold probably learned about Stansbury's availability as a courier from his bride; Peggy, in turn, would have known about the man through her relationship with Captain John Andre.

Stansbury accepted Arnold's statement and left for New York the next morning. Arnold's message was simple: he would "help to defeat the American rebels" and restore America to the British Empire. With help from a Loyalist minister named Jonathan Odell, Stansbury went to British Headquarters, where he met with General Clinton's adjutant, John Andre, now a major, who had just become head of Clinton's secret service.

Andre must have been stunned by Stansbury's message, and not surprisingly, he proceeded with considerable caution. In fact, over the next five months the Andre-Arnold correspondence involved the two men trying to find ways to trust one another while also gaining their respective goals. One of the first steps was to arrange a system of secret communication. Both men would have the two books on which a code was based: primarily Blackstone's *Commentaries* and also Bailey's *Dictionary*. The code was made of three digits, indicating 1) the page number, 2) the line number, and 3) the word number. An alternative involved using invisible ink, with "A" designating acid for decoding, or "F" for fire (heat).

However, Andre apparently wanted to have greater assurance of secrecy, so he involved Peggy in the correspondence. He suggested that "The lady might write to me at the same time with one of her intimates. She will guess who I mean, the latter remaining ignorant of interlining and sending the letter. I will write myself to the friend to give occasion for a reply." 17. The friend chosen was Peggy Chew, who was Peggy Arnold's closest friend and had also acted in an extravaganza designed by Andre (part of a huge farewell celebration at the time of the British departure from Philadelphia). [Peggy Shippen was forbidden from participating by her father who said the costume designed by Andre was too revealing.]

From May 1779 to October the communication between Andre and Arnold became a slow dance of disappointment and frustration for both sides. First, the exchange of messages was extremely dangerous. Stansbury and Odell could not always deliver messages in person, so trustworthy men or women had to be found. The letters between Peggy Chew and Andre were exchanged under a flag of truce, as was done for normally innocent letters. These, and other matters, often meant a delay of up to six weeks between the sending of a letter and a response.

Most troubling was the failure of either side to obtain satisfaction from the other. Arnold wanted some assurance that he would receive at least a minimum sum for his betrayal; he asked Clinton for assurance of 10,000 pounds. Clinton, however, was reluctant to make a commitment until he was certain that Arnold was serious and could offer something substantial. One suggestion from Andre was that Arnold rejoin Washington's army, obtain a field command, and then manage to surrender five or six thousand men. Andre also suggested that a field command could make possible a meeting between Arnold and himself which, he felt certain, would satisfy both sides.

By October, Arnold was fed up. He had frequently sent information to Andre about troop movements, the location of the French fleet and army, plus other matters, but nothing led Clinton to make a commitment of money. Benedict broke off all communication with the British. It was not until May of the following year (1780) that he was willing to try again. Peggy continued to correspond with Andre, mostly on matters of fabrics and accessories that he could obtain for her.

By the autumn of 1779, then, little had been accomplished, except that Arnold had crossed his Rubicon into a land of betrayal. How could he turn back? If he ever took a field command against the British, they would simply expose his communication with Andre and the game would be up. He had maneuvered himself into a most uncomfortable situation.

Unanswered Questions

One of the most difficult questions about Arnold's decision to become a traitor is why he chose May of 1779 to commit himself. He had just married Peggy Shippen and had recently purchased the beautiful estate of Mount Pleasant. While it's true that his trial had been postponed until January, he did not have to rush. Why not take advantage of the long delay? They could have settled into married life, enjoyed their new home, and Benedict could have taken time to go to New York to try to work out the state's generous offer.

At nearly the same time, Arnold wrote his frenzied letter to Washington when the commander agreed to delay Benedict's trial. How could delay of the trial be "worse than death"? And the trial itself was not going to involve anything so serious as to require Benedict Arnold's execution.

Somehow in that month of May events seemed to speed up in Arnold's mind to a frantic pace—the marriage, the new trial, Washington's postponement of it, and Benedict's anguished letter. One wonders why these events led to treason within three weeks of the wedding.

Is it possible that Benedict's marriage to Peggy was an important factor? Most historians and biographers have not thought so. Some have not even mentioned her possible influence on his decision. However, the simple matter of timing makes it worth exploring. She certainly would have felt deeply for her new husband's anguish so expressed in his letter to Washington. She had close friends among the British, and she probably was aware that shopkeeper Stansbury would make a perfect go-between. It would seem only natural for her to urge him to ease his suffering by at least talking with someone in the British camp. Is there proof? The full discussion of her involvement, and the evidence, is in Chapter Thirteen.

CHAPTER ELEVEN

# The Tortured Road To Betrayal

AFTER HE BROKE OFF COMMUNICATION WITH Major John Andre in October, 1779, Benedict lived through more than six months of turmoil, frustration, and isolation. He became more desperate than ever to restore his reputation and to gain financial stability. He may have been motivated by the quixotic notion that, if successful in these efforts, he could simply drop the plan to join the British. Apparently he was not concerned about the British exposing his steps toward treason, since he had spent much of his life fighting off accusations.

From October to the following May, however, nothing went Arnold's way. Reed and his Council of Pennsylvania attacked him relentlessly. Congress continued to treat him shabbily, and his finances became more, not less, tangled.

## "Fort Wilson" and Isolation

An incident in the autumn of 1779 made Benedict feel both alone and in danger. By October, a steady decline in the value of Continental currency, combined with the French army's purchases of local farm produce, led to severe food shortages in Philadelphia. Bands of disgruntled men began roaming the streets, seeking those they thought were profiting from the skyrocketing prices. When a number of those suspected were harried by a large armed mob, they fled to the home of James Wilson.

There were soon about thirty men barricaded in what they called "Fort Wilson." Most of the men were staunch Patriots, and three of them, including Wilson, were signers of the Declaration of Independence. Benedict Arnold came to help and took command of defense on the second floor; General Thomas Mifflin directed on the first floor.

The defenders turned back the first attack after a brisk exchange of musket fire. The mob suffered about twenty casualties, including four killed; a few defenders suffered minor injuries. The mob regrouped and attacked again, battering down the front door, and bayoneting one defender before retreating. The attackers were preparing for their third assault when Continental troops arrived and the emergency was over.

Arnold, however, remained a target of anger. People in the street yelled at him and threw stones at his carriage. When a crowd gathered around the Arnold home, he dashed off a note to Congress asking for Continentals to protect him and his family. In a curt message, Congress refused to help and advised him that he should have turned to "the executive authority of the state of Pennsylvania" (Joseph Reed and Co.), adding that Congress had full confidence in the state's ability "to protect every honest citizen . . . and highly disapprove the insulations of every individual to the contrary." 1. Arnold had asked for help for an "honest citizen" which the state government could not seem to provide.

Although Arnold apologized for the "misunderstanding," and local authorities managed to disperse the crowd, he was deeply shaken. First, he had been disappointed in his dangerous negotiations with the British. Next, he found himself still battling with Joseph Reed and his Council who were clearly determined to destroy him. Now he found that, even with his life threatened, he had no friends in Congress. Feeling isolated and humiliated was bad enough, but that was just the beginning. Joseph Reed and his council, as well as Congress, were about to make matters worse.

## The Long Court Battle

As early as February, 1779, the Pennsylvania Council had brought eight charges against Benedict Arnold when he was on his way to meet with General Schuyler in New York. Reed wanted the trial held in a state court, and for maximum exposure he had copies of the charges sent to Congress, General Washington, and authorities in every state, as well as every major newspaper. Since the charges, including several hearings before Congress and two trials, were not settled for a year, the public had time to consider the Council's statement that

Arnold was " . . . oppressive to the faithful subjects of this state, unworthy of his rank and station, highly discouraging to those who have manifested their attachment to the liberties and interests of America, and disrespectful to the supreme executive authority." 2.

Joseph Reed made matters worse by charging that Arnold "fled" the state *after* the charges were made, not before, making it clear that he was trying to elude the trial. Reed and his Council were determined to bring Arnold down, and there were plenty of shady dealings that he was guilty of. The Council's problem was that their eight charges were simply too flimsy. Some charges were merely statements of their intense dislike of the man; for example, that he had made "an indecent and disrespectful refusal" to explain the use of public wagons; and that he showed favoritism to Loyalists. Regarding the few charges that might have hurt Arnold, they could find no evidence.

Although the case against Arnold seemed so weak, the matter dragged on for a year. He continually defended himself with righteous indignation; or, as Van Doren stated it: "Arnold, who was more guilty than the council could know, denied any guilt with his usual bold vigor." 3.

The Council was fortunate that Congress did not dare clamp down on the case because they could not afford to antagonize Pennsylvania. Nevertheless, the congressional committee to which the charges were submitted repeatedly asked for evidence, and when there was none, were forced to dismiss most of the charges for lack of evidence. Two charges regarding the use of public wagons were to be turned over to Washington for a court-martial.

At first, Arnold was pleased and wrote to Congress his hope for a speedy trial. Washington set a date of May 1, 1779, but Reed's objections led to delays so that he could contact witnesses and gather evidence. The delays led Benedict to write his frenzied letter ("Delay . . . is worse than death") to Washington. Finally, in June, advances by the British forced a postponement until the campaigning season was over. Not until late December, 1779, did the court-martial finally hold hearings in Morristown, New Jersey.

The main charges against him involved using public wagons to move private goods and allowing a trading vessel (the *Charming Nancy*) to clear port when others were denied. Benedict's defense was eloquent and persuasive, especially his opening statement:

> When the present necessary war against Great Britain commenced, I was in easy circumstances and enjoyed a fair prospect of improving them. I was happy in domestic connections and blessed with a rising family who claimed my care and attention. The liberties of my country were in danger. The voice of my country called upon all her faithful sons to join in her defense. With cheerfulness, I obeyed the call. I sacrificed domestic ease and happiness to the service of my country, and in her service have I sacrificed a great part of a handsome fortune. I was one of the first who appeared in the field and, from that time to the present hour, have not abandoned her service.

Arnold then responded to all of the original eight charges against him, saying that he considered the attacks against him by Reed and his Council to be "a vile prostitution of power." Referring to the charge that he had closed the city's shops but arranged to make large purchases for his own uses, he claimed that, if guilty, he would be "the vilest of men." He concluded, "The blood I have spent in defence of my country will be insufficient to obliterate the stain." 4.

In typical Benedict Arnold fashion, he did not mention that he had, in fact, profited from closing the shops. He was fortunate that Reed and his Council could not find his secret correspondence with the two men who shared the sales and profits with him.

The court-martial delivered its verdict on January 26, 1780. The officers found only that his use of public wagons was "imprudent and improper" and sentenced him "to receive a reprimand from his Excellency the commander-in-chief." 5.

Through the months of feeling betrayed and isolated, Benedict had held out the hope that Washington would always stand by him. Now, with the court's decision so humiliating, he thought that the commander-in-chief might ignore the verdict, or merely say a few words in private. Even the men of the Pennsylvania Council seemed to feel that Arnold had already suffered more than a man could bear. In an unusual letter to Congress, the Council wrote,

"We find his sufferings for, and services to, his country so deeply impressed upon our minds as to obliterate every opposing sentiment, and therefore beg leave to request that Congress will be pleased to dispense with the part of the sentence which imposes a public censure, and may most affect the feelings of a brave and gallant officer." 6.

Arnold endured more delays by Congress; the court-martial verdict was delivered in January, but it was April before Congress sent its report to Washington. And the commander-in-chief took seriously the court's verdict which required him to issue a reprimand and he decided it must be a public statement. In fact, the reprimand became famous for its statement of ethics in the military:

> Our profession is the chastest of all. Even the shadow of a fault tarnishes the luster of our finest achievements. The least inadvertence may rob us of the public favor so hard to be acquired. I reprimand you for having forgotten that, in proportion as you have made yourself formidable to your enemies, you should have been guarded and temperate in your deportment toward your fellow citizens. Exhibit anew those qualities which have placed you on the list of our most valued commanders. 7.

## The Tangled Web of Finances

While Benedict suffered through a year of confusion and humiliation leading to the court-martial verdict, he also struggled with Congress over his finances during the same year, from April 1779 to April 1780. The seemingly endless hearings, reports, and rumors led General Charles Lee to comment that Arnold "was served up as a constant dish of scandal to the breakfast of every table on the continent . . . in this general rage for abuse." 8.

Beginning in April 1779, the attempt to straighten out Arnold's finances was bounced between Congress and the Board of the Treasury. No one seemed willing or able to deal with the complexities. After months of wrangling, the Treasury Board did allow Arnold a credit of $51,993, but refused to grant an additional $3,300. In the final analysis of all the accounts, the Board concluded that Arnold owed the United States a balance of $2,328 for the Canadian Campaign.

The Board's report, issued on April 27, 1780 infuriated Arnold, and he demanded an appeal, arguing that members of the Treasury Board had engaged in a vendetta against him. His anger, and his insistence on the additional $3,300 owed him above the $51,9993 already granted has led some writers to conclude that he was in desperate need of money.

Recent biographers have disputed the conclusion that the need for money was a major motive for his decision to turn to the British. For example, Jim Murphy argues that Benedict's finances were not desperate. He points out that Congress still owed him pay for nearly four years of military service; he was also owed money for various business dealings. The total owed him came to 12,000 pounds, which he could never collect if he turned traitor. Also, his homes, property, warehouses, carriages, and horses would all be confiscated by state and national governments. In other words, Murphy concludes, Arnold stood to lose large sums by turning traitor.

Congress did act on Arnold's appeal in May 1780, appointing a three-man committee to consider his appeal and the report of the Board. There was no final resolution of the financial tangle.

**What Led to Full-Fledged Treason?**

In May 1780, Benedict renewed contact with the British through Stansbury, and in early June wrote that he expected to be placed in command of West Point. The Hudson River complex of forts, it turned out, had become central to Arnold's planning. He was now dedicating himself to helping America's enemy, by giving them the key to the nation's defenses.

Why did he suddenly recommit himself to treachery? If money was not the motive, what other factors were involved? The following are major elements described by biographers and historians:

First, throughout his long struggle with Congress, the Board of the Treasury, and the Executive Council of Pennsylvania, he achieved few victories to counter-balance the endless assaults on his pride. One of the rare moments of happiness was the birth of his son, Edward, on March 19, 1780.

When Washington issued his reprimand, which he regarded as extremely mild, Arnold was crushed. This has been seen by several writers as the last straw for Benedict; the one person he had always counted on appeared to have turned against him, accepting the accusations of Joseph Reed over Arnold's often-emotional defenses. His feelings of isolation and humiliation were so deep it could have created a powerful desire for revenge.

Second, in the critical years of 1779 and 1780, the American Revolution seemed to be on the brink of failure. The patriotic enthusiasm that had brought out tens of thousands of militia volunteers to fight for independence in 1775 had been dissipated by years of warfare, shortages, and failure of leadership. The army, which had numbered more than 27,000 in 1775 was reduced to less than 3,500 by 1780.

The plight of the army in the winter of 1779-1780 was even worse than at Valley Forge. A committee of Congress, headed by General Schuyler, reported on May 10 that the soldiers were losing patience and that "their starving condition, their want of pay, and the variety of hardship they have been driven to sustain, has soured their tempers, and produced a spirit of discontent which begins to display itself under a complexion of the most alarming hue." 9.

One of the soldiers—Joseph Plumb Martin—described conditions in less flowery terms; by 1780:

> We . . . still kept upon the parade in groups, venting our spleen at our country and government, then at our officers, and then at our imbecility in staying there and starving in detail for an ungrateful people who did not care what became of us, so they could enjoy themselves while we were keeping a cruel enemy from them. 10.

Many Patriot leaders were convinced that the failures of Congress were bringing the country close to collapse. General Washington, in a letter to a Congressman, wrote that he was "certain . . . that unless Congress speaks in a more decisive tone; unless they are vested with powers by the several states . . . or assume them as a matter of right; and they, and the states respectively, act with more energy . . . that our Cause is lost." 11. James Madison added that Congress had become so weak that "They can neither enlist, pay nor feed a single soldier, nor execute any other purpose but as the means are first put in their hands." 12.

Since this was the Congress that had treated Benedict badly on so many occasions, he may have come to feel that the well-mannered British would treat him with greater respect. In addition, the royal treasury had real money, not the rapidly-depleting Continental currency. Another temptation for Arnold could have been the act of Parliament, passed in January 1779, offering to grant all the Americans' demands short of independence. This would enable Benedict to picture himself as the great peace maker.

Many others had also become disillusioned with the Patriot cause and large numbers turned to the British. Deserters, called "scuffs," often left to help their families or to avoid starvation. By 1780, growing numbers joined Loyalist militia. Major General Nathanael Greene wrote to Virginia Governor Thomas Jefferson to report that much of the state had sided with the British. "The enemy," he said, "have raised seven independent companies in a single day and we have the mortification to find that most of the prisoners we take are inhabitants of America." 13.

Several writers have suggested that Arnold's distrust of France was a contributing factor in his decision. Many Americans were also suspicious of what the French would do when and if the British were defeated. The Loyalist *Royal Gazette* in New York printed an article that was circulated throughout New England, warning that, as soon as French troops landed, revolutionary governments would quickly give way to "the establishment of the French government, laws and customs. . . ." 14.

However, as Carl Van Doren commented in his *Secret History of the American Revolution*: "In spite of Arnold's later claim that he had been opposed to independence and the French alliance, he seems never to have put a syllable of dissatisfaction on record anywhere before May 1779." 15.

There are, then, a number of factors that could have influenced Benedict's ultimate decision: the signs that the Revolution was failing; the weakness of Congress and the Pennsylvania Council, including their unfair treatment of Arnold; the feeling that Washington had betrayed him; distrust of the French, contrasted with the British willingness to grant Americans everything they demanded, except independence. In addition, his need, or desire, for money cannot be entirely ruled out, in spite of the evidence that he was owed an even greater sum than he was demanding from the British. He had lost an important source of income when he stepped down as military governor during his long court battle. At the same time, his courtship and marriage had increased his expenses considerably. And, throughout his life, most of the conflicts he was engaged in involved money in some way.

In trying to sort through all of the factors operating in Arnold's tortured mind, one is struck by the feeling that no combination of these elements offers a satisfactory explanation for the greatest betrayal in America's history. But, when combined with the weaknesses in Benedict's character, the picture becomes clearer.

### Benedict's Character Flaws

Benedict Arnold is regarded as one of the great battlefield leaders in our history—brave to the point of recklessness, an inspiration to his men, and possessing a unique ability to respond quickly in any military emergency. But he was not a great man. Other leading figures, including Washington, Jefferson, and Franklin, had suffered frequently at the hands of political enemies, but they all held on to their larger vision of winning independence.

Many contemporary observers as well as modern writers, have felt that Arnold's self-confidence often spilled over into arrogance. This frequently led him to react to any charges as nothing but personal attacks. He had a remarkable ability to deny—apparently even to himself—that he was at fault in any way.

This confidence could also lead to an inflated sense of his own value or importance. When he first opened negotiations with Major Andre, for example, he chose the code name "Monk," a reference to George Monk, a 17th century English general who switched sides after the death of Oliver Cromwell and restored the monarchy (Charles II), becoming a great patriotic hero in the process. Arnold could picture himself as a new patriot, changing sides to restore America to its proper place within the British Empire. He was certain that thousands would follow his lead.

Benedict was also convinced that his services and sacrifices for his country warranted special consideration. Throughout the almost endless hearings and trials, he made frequent reference to his having become a cripple in his service to the cause of independence. He used his disability to gain his goals, most significantly when he told Washington he could not accept a field command but could manage the command of West Point.

At one point in his court battles, he came up with the idea of forming a naval expedition to the West Indies. In order to obtain Washington's permission for three or four hundred troops, he managed to give the impression that the initiative had come from the Board of Admiralty. The plan flopped quickly when Washington decided he could not spare the men and the Admiralty Board also dropped it. However, the episode revealed Arnold's tendency to bend the truth to suit his purposes.

Finally, as biographer Willard Wallace noted, "He was a pathetic case of insecurity." He desperately wanted to be accepted as an equal by the "first families." But, "one of his obsessions was that riches ensured respectability and that the means by which those riches were gained was immaterial." 16.

There is no way to measure how each of these potential motivations worked on Benedict's flawed character. One other element involves the possible role of his wife Peggy. Modern writers have been convinced that she was involved in the treason but could not have influenced the decision of someone as strong willed as Arnold. Analyzing her actions in the next two chapters will clarify the picture.

# CHAPTER TWELVE

# "Treason of the Blackest Dye"

IN MAY 1780, BENEDICT MADE HIS DECISION to re-open negotiations with Major Andre and General Clinton. The coded messages bounced back and forth through the summer until Arnold and Andre arranged for a secret meeting in September.

For this round of negotiations, Benedict decided to offer a prize Clinton would have to find exciting: he would have himself appointed the commandant of West Point and then turn it over to the British for a sum of at least 20,000 pounds. West Point quickly became the centerpiece of the exchanges.

## The West Point Fixation

West Point was a string of four major forts, plus a blockhouse, and several hilltop fortifications stretching for fifteen miles along the lower Hudson River, guarding the river and the 1,097-foot-long chain designed to prevent British warships from sailing upriver. General Washington often referred to West Point as "the Key to America." With the French now establishing their base at Rhode Island and Washington's army in New Jersey, West Point provided a connecting link for communication and troop movements. In British hands, however, America would be cut in two.

In May or June, Arnold notified Andre and Clinton that he expected to be appointed to the command of West Point. At the same time, he wrote to his friend Schuyler, hinting that he was interested in the post. Schuyler's reply is lost, but in early June, after a meeting with Washington, he reported to Benedict:

> He [Washington] expressed a desire to do whatever was agreeable to you, dwelt on your abilities, your merits, your sufferings and on the well-earned claims you have on your

country, and intimated that as soon as his arrangements for the campaign should take place that he would properly consider you. I believe you will have an alternative proposal, either to take charge of an important post, with an honourable command, or your station in the field. Your reputation, my dear sir, so established, your honourable scars, put it decidedly in your power to take either. A state [NY] . . . will wish to see its banners entrusted to you. If the command at West Point is offered, it will be honourable; if a division in the field, you must judge whether you can support the fatigues, circumstanced as you are. 1.

In typical Benedict Arnold fashion, he interpreted Schuyler's conjecture to mean that Washington was promising that West Point was his. On June 12, Arnold met with Washington in Morristown, but there is no record of what was said; on the same day, however, he wrote to the British that "Mr. Moore [his new code name] expects to have the command of West Point" 2. offered to him by early July. Washington was intending to launch a full campaign against New York, with French help, and he had wanted to give Arnold command of the entire left wing of the army. After both Schuyler and New York Congressman Robert Livingston wrote to Washington urging him to give West Point to Benedict, Washington finally agreed.

By mid-July, Benedict was on his way to West Point, after asking Congress for money in advance of the four years' pay he was owed. Congress advanced him $25,000, and as he left Philadelphia for the last time, he was hoping to acquire an even larger sum from Clinton.

## The Greatest Treachery

Arnold had a huge scare on August 1, when he met with Washington while part of the army was crossing the Hudson at King's Ferry. The commander-in-chief was so eager to close in on New York that he again offered his fighting general command of the army's left wing. Arnold was shocked when Washington's General Orders announced from Peekskill that the army's left wing was to be commanded by Major General Benedict Arnold.

The matter was finally straightened out and Arnold was soon safely settled in the house of Beverley Robinson, Benedict's new headquarters, across the river from West Point. It would be interesting to know what was going on in his mind as he wiggled out of what should have been the promotion of a lifetime. The man who was devoted to action and longed to restore his family's honor would have been in command of one-third of the army in what could have been the decisive campaign of the war. All that was now being swept away by his betrayal. Did he consider accepting the promotion, then plan to deny any accusations the British might make? Probably not, considering what the next incident reveals about how far he had fallen into heinous treachery.

On September 15, 1780, Benedict received a letter from Washington with a confidential postscript:

> I shall be at Peekskill on Sunday evening, on my way to Hartford to meet the French Admiral [Ternay] and General [Rochambeau]. You will be pleased to send down a guard of a captain and 50 at that time, and direct the quartermaster to have a night's forage for about 40 horses. You will keep this to yourself, as I want to keep my journey a secret. 3.

Arnold immediately replied to the commander that the guard and forage would be provided. At the same time, he wrote a cipher letter to Clinton: "General Washington will be at King's Ferry Sunday evening next on his way to Hartford to meet the French Admiral and General. And will lodge at Peekskill." 4.

That was an astounding betrayal, even for Benedict Arnold. He was willing to give up the country's most important leader, and a man who had been his mentor and who had admired and trusted him through years of turmoil. The British already had a sloop of war, the *Vulture*, in the Hudson not far from Peekskill, with others available, making a river attack quite possible. No attempt to capture Washington took place—either because the timing was off or Clinton did not have complete confidence in Arnold yet. In either case, no one ever knew of this black spot in Benedict's heart until Clinton's papers were made available after 1900.

## Finalizing Plans

By August, Benedict had assured Major Andre and General Clinton that he planned to be in command at West Point and would then turn it over to the British for 20,000 pounds. Sir Henry was thrilled by the idea. If Washington attacked New York, the British could move up the Hudson, take control of the West Point complex and then push south, driving the Americans into Virginia. Like Arnold, Clinton was confident that thousands of rebels would follow Arnold's lead and restore their loyalty to the Crown.

Two problems stood in the way of completing the deal: Communications between New York and West Point became increasingly difficult, and Clinton was cautious about trusting Arnold. He continually refused to agree to the sum Benedict asked for and wanted some proof of his intentions, such as arranging the capture of 5,000-6,000 American troops, or gaining the release of Burgoyne's Saratoga forces still being kept prisoner. For Benedict's part, the American turncoat insisted on knowing exactly how much he would receive.

By mid-August, Clinton was ready to take a chance, but first he wanted a meeting between Arnold and Andre to finalize the details. Problems with communication and logistics forced delays until late September.

Just before the scheduled meeting, Arnold was thrilled by the arrival of Peggy and their infant son. He had planned for her journey with great care, sending his aide, Major David Franks, to Philadelphia to bring her north. Arnold had carefully listed each of the six overnight stops they would make and even suggested that a feather bed in a wagon would be more comfortable for Peggy and their son than a closed carriage. Benedict Arnold biographer Willard Wallace observed: "Arnold was overjoyed to have Peggy with him again and not simply as a co-conspirator. After weeks of separation, their reunion had the element of a honeymoon but one spiced with knowledge of the dangerous game they were playing." 5.

In the effort to bring Andre to Arnold, there were several missteps in the early weeks of September. At one point, as Arnold was being rowed south to meet Andre at Dobbs Ferry, his barge was fired on by the British; Arnold was nearly killed but managed to get away. The often-delayed meeting was rescheduled for the night of September 21.

## The Andre-Arnold Meeting

In the long cast of characters in the saga of Benedict Arnold, John Andre is one of the most fascinating and compelling figures. In a 1902 introduction to Andre's journal, Henry Cabot Lodge offered this description of the man:

> There is a pleasant tinge of romance about the man himself, for he was young, handsome, and possessed of many accomplishments, clever, agreeable, popular. . . . The favorite of his commanders, a trusted staff-officer, advancing easily along the road to promotion, beloved among his fellows, popular in Society, he passes suddenly out of the sunshine of a young prosperity into the darkness of a desperate enterprise, becomes the paymaster of treason, a disguised fugitive, a prisoner, a convicted spy, and dies at last by the hangman's hand. 6.

On the night of September 21, the conspirators planned to meet at the home of Joshua Smith on the banks of the Hudson, about 15 miles south of West Point. Smith, who knew nothing of the conspiracy, was rowed to the *Vulture* by two of his tenant farmers and picked up a "businessman" named John Anderson, the code name Andre had used from the beginning. Andre wore his British uniform, but it was completely hidden by a cape. (Clinton had warned him to stay in uniform, or he could be executed as a spy if caught behind American lines.)

Andre and Arnold finally met around midnight at Smith's home. Few details of the meeting are known, but Arnold did give him his written analysis of the fort along with details about where the defenses were weakest. He probably also mentioned that Washington would be stopping at the fort on Monday. Since the meeting had lasted past four a.m. on Friday, and Smith had no rowers available, the men decided to wait until nightfall to have new rowers take Andre to the *Vulture*, Since Smith knew Mr. Anderson only as a New York businessman, he felt no rush to return him to the *Vulture*.

The delay in leaving Smith's residence until after dark on Friday did not seem to matter. But as so often happened with Arnold's schemes, fate stepped in and changed everything. During the day on Friday, Patriot officers opened fire on the *Vulture* from shore batteries, without orders from Arnold, inflicting a good deal of damage. The sloop's captain ordered his ship south about ten miles, leaving Andre behind at Smith's home.

Benedict decided that Andre would have to make his way to New York by land, with Smith accompanying him part of the way. Arnold wrote a pass for him in case he was stopped by a Patriot patrol. Andre also had to change out of his British uniform, since they would be traveling by day.

While Benedict headed north to West Point on Friday, Smith and Andre started their ride south. About nine o'clock, they were stopped by a patrol of New York State militia. The captain of the militia warned them that they were entering a no man's land where bands of armed Loyalists called "Cowboys" roamed, eager to capture any Patriots, and other bands of Patriot militia, known as "Skinners," were eager to make prisoners of any Loyalists. They followed the captain's suggestion and spent the night in a farmhouse, and left again early Saturday.

When Andre and Smith reached the bridge over the Croton River, Smith suddenly announced that he was turning back. Forced to continue alone, Andre took the road along the Hudson and had reached within a half-mile of the safety of Tarrytown, when three armed men came out of the woods and ordered him to stop. Seeing that one of the men wore a Hessian soldier's green coat, Andre told them that he was with "the lower party"—meaning a Loyalist from New York. The leader, John Paulding, simply nodded and Andre, thinking he was safe, said, "Thank God, I am among friends, I am glad to see you. I am an officer in the British service, and have now been on particular business in the country, and I hope you will not detain me." 7.

Paulding suddenly grabbed the bridle of Andre's horse and ordered him to climb down. Too late, Andre realized he had ridden into a trap. If he had said nothing and simply produced his pass he probably would not have been detained. Instead, Paulding said, "We are Americans," and led him into the woods to search him for money. Andre tried to correct the situation. He showed them Arnold's pass and warned the Skinners not to detain him on the general's business.

Nothing worked for the desperate spy. They searched his clothes, his saddle and his equipment, then ordered him to take off his boots. They nearly missed the three wrapped papers in his sock, and, when they removed them, could not figure out what they were.

The Skinners figured they had caught a spy and decided they should take him to a militia officer for a possible reward. They ordered Andre to get dressed, tied his hands behind his back, and lifted him onto his horse. They led him to a guard post at North Castle and turned him over to Colonel John Jameson. One of the three militia men later recalled how suddenly Andre's mood had changed. "You never saw such an alteration in any man's face. Only a few moments before, he was uncommonly gay in his looks, but after we made him prisoner, you could read in his face that he thought it was all over with him." 8.

Colonel Jameson did not know what to do with the prisoner or the papers. He did not suspect that Arnold was leading a conspiracy, so he planned to send Andre to Arnold at West Point, along with copies of the papers; the original of the papers were to go to Washington, who was known to be coming from Hartford.

Major Benjamin Tallmadge, who was second in command at North Castle, knew that Arnold had been planning to meet a man named Anderson. He now figured that it was Anderson who was caught taking papers *away* from West Point, and he urged Jameson to have "Anderson" brought back to North Castle and not to tell Arnold. Jameson did not feel right accusing Benedict of being a traitor; he did agree to have Andre brought back to North Castle but also insisted on sending a note to Arnold telling him of the capture.

Benedict spent a quiet weekend at home with Peggy. They could feel good about their plan, especially after Smith sent word that Andre was safely on his way. General Washington, along with Alexander Hamilton and General Lafayette were expected Monday morning, but that should be an easy scene for Peggy and Arnold to play. However, the messages Jameson sent to Washington and to Arnold did not arrive until Monday and that was when the world of the three conspirators exploded.

**Exposure and Flight**

On Monday morning, Alexander Hamilton and another aide arrived at Benedict's headquarters and announced that Washington would be delayed and to go ahead with the breakfast without him. Breakfast had just started when Jameson's messenger arrived with the note describing Andre's capture. Arnold read the note at the door, swore the man to secrecy, and sent him to join the others.

Minutes later, Arnold rushed upstairs where he told Peggy that Andre had been captured. He had to try to get away to the *Vulture* ahead of Washington's men. Since there was no way to take Peggy and Neddy with him, Arnold had to tell her how to answer the questions they were bound to ask. They both seemed confident that she could manage her way out of the situation.

Peggy stayed in their room while Benedict limped downstairs, ordering that a horse be saddled immediately. He told Franks to inform Washington that he had been called over to the Point but would be back in about an hour. Riding at a reckless pace, Arnold took a shortcut down a steep incline that became known as Traitor's Hill to the Hudson River landing. His barge and eight oarsmen were as always ready. He ordered the men to row with greatest speed down river to the *Vulture*. Within a short time, Arnold raised a white flag and climbed safely on board the sloop. He offered his crewmen promotions and bonuses if they would join the British. All refused.

Less than a half-hour after Arnold fled his headquarters, Washington arrived at the Robinson House across from West Point. The commander had seemed in a good mood, joking with his aides when they chafed about a detour. "I know you young men are all in love with Mrs. Arnold," he said and told them they could ride ahead if they wished. 9.

After breakfast, Washington, Lafayette and Knox crossed to West Point, planning to meet with Arnold. Arnold, of course, was not there, and Washington was disturbed to see that the defenses were in a sorry state of disrepair. He returned to the Robinson House and went to the room assigned to him to rest. Minutes later Hamilton came in with the packet of papers from Colonel Jameson, including Arnold's assessment of West Point and Andre's letter to Washington in which he confessed his identity.

Washington read the documents in stunned silence. His bravest, most reliable officer had sold out to the British. Lafayette later recalled entering the room and seeing Washington sitting on the bed, holding the papers in trembling hands. "Arnold has betrayed me," he muttered. "Whom can we trust now?" 10.

Even in shock, Washington maintained his famous ability to act calmly. He ordered Hamilton and McHenry to try to catch Arnold before he reached the *Vulture*. But the traitor had too great a head start.

Once Arnold was safely on board the war sloop, he quickly relaxed enough to write to Washington, saying that "I have ever acted from a principle of love to my country. . . . The same principle of love to my country actuates my present conduct, however it may appear inconsistent to the world, who very seldom judge right of any man's actions." Benedict also tried to assure the commander that Peggy was not involved in the conspiracy and had no knowledge of it. He asked Washington to protect her "from every insult and injury that a mistaken vengeance of my country may expose her to. . . . [She] is as good and innocent as an angel, and is incapable of doing wrong." 11.

### First Reactions

While Hamilton and McHenry tried to catch up with Arnold, Washington set to work to bring army regiments to the Hudson Valley, and had work crews begin to strengthen the fort complex. The commander-in-chief also questioned Benedict's aides – Varick and Franks – not because he thought they were guilty, but to gain any information they might have about Arnold's movements. Both men were placed under arrest, but Washington assured them that this was merely a formality.

The general also wanted to talk to Peggy, but soon after Arnold made his escape, she suffered through several hours of hysterics and sobbing, at times appearing to be quite out of her mind. She asked to see Washington, but when he entered her room, she hysterically denied it was the general. Washington quietly left.

Convinced of her innocence, Washington later told her through an aide, that "though my duty required that no means should be neglected to arrest General Arnold, I have the great pleasure in acquainting *her* that he is now safe." 12 The General told Peggy she was free to leave, and she would be escorted either to New York and her husband, or to her family in Philadelphia. She chose Philadelphia, and by nightfall on September 27 – the day after Arnold's escape – she was on her way with Major Franks as her guide. The hysterics had apparently subsided.

Peggy's theatrics, either actual hysterics or brilliant acting, had convinced everyone of her innocence. A more detailed account of her story is presented in the next chapter.

Also on the morning of the 27th, General Greene's General Orders broke the news to a shocked nation: "*Treason* of the blackest dye was yesterday discovered! General Arnold, who commanded at West Point, lost to every sentiment of honor, of public and private obligation, was about to deliver up that important post into the hands of the enemy. Such an event must have given the American cause a deadly wound, if not a fatal stab. Happily, the treason has been timely discovered to prevent the fatal misfortune. The providential train of circumstances which led to it affords the most convincing proof that the liberties of America are the object of divine protection. . . .

"His Excellency, the Commander-in-Chief, has arrived at West Point . . . and is no doubt taking the proper measures to unravel fully so hellish a plot." 13.

## The Death of Major Andre

Of the many strange circumstances in the treason of Benedict Arnold, perhaps the most remarkable was the tragedy of Major Andre. From the day of his capture, Andre won the admiration and sympathy of a steadily growing number of people.

He was first taken to West Point where he was questioned by Washington and his staff. He was then rowed back down the Hudson to Stony Point, where a large escort of mounted soldiers took him to Tappan where he was imprisoned at Mabie's Tavern. A board of fourteen officers was convened to examine Andre and to render a verdict.

The prisoner admitted to having the papers on his person and to traveling in disguise, but vehemently denied being a common spy. He insisted he had arrived in uniform and fully expected to be rowed back to the *Vulture* in uniform. But Benedict refused and Andre thus became a prisoner.

After a brief deliberation, the board issued its unanimous decision "that Major Andre, adjutant general to the British army ought to be considered as a spy from the enemy; and that, agreeable to the law and usage of nations, it is [our] opinion he ought to suffer death." 14. The execution was set for Sunday, October 1, at noon.

Everyone seemed deeply moved by the announcement of the sentence. When told of his fate, Andre was momentarily stunned but quickly regained his composure. Major Tallmadge, who had gone with Andre to West Point and then to Tappan, said he remained as cheerful as if he was going to [a meeting] . . . . I am sure he will go to the gallows less fearful for his fate and with less concern than I shall behold the tragedy." 15.

The Marquis de Lafayette visited Andre on the day of the execution. Lafayette reported that, "he conducted himself in a manner so frank, so delicate that . . . I had the foolishness to let myself acquire a strong affection for him." 16.

On the day of the execution, Andre's breakfast was sent to him from General Washington's table, as had been done every day. When his personal servant came in in tears, Andre said, "Leave me until you can show yourself more manly." After eating, shaving, and dressing, he told the guard-officers he was ready.

Dr. Thacher, who had kept a highly detailed journal throughout the Revolution, described the solemn scene:

> The fatal hour having arrived, a large detachment of troops was paraded and an immense concourse of people assembled. Almost all our general and field-officers, excepting his Excellency and his staff, were present on horseback. Melancholy and gloom pervaded all ranks, and the scene was awfully affecting. I was so near, during the solemn march to the fatal spot, as to observe every emotion the melancholy scene was calculated to produce. Major Andre walked from the stone house . . . between two of our subaltern officers, arm in arm. The eyes of the immense multitude were fixed on him, who,

rising superior to the fears of death, appeared as if conscious of
the dignified deportment he displayed. He betrayed no want
of fortitude, but retained a complacent smile . . . and politely
bowed to several gentlemen whom he knew, which was re-
spectfully returned.

Andre had appealed to be executed by firing squad and he was disappointed
when he learned it was to be death by hanging. "I am reconciled to my death,"
he said, "but I detest the mode."

As soon as he saw that everything was ready, he stepped
quickly into the wagon. At this moment he appeared to
shrink; but instantly elevating his head with firmness, he
said, 'It will be but a momentary pang'; and taking from his
pocket two white handkerchiefs, the provost-marshal with
one loosely pinioned his arms, and with the other the victim . . . bandaged his own eyes with perfect firmness, which
melted the hearts and moistened the cheeks . . . of the throng
of spectators. The rope being appended to the gallows, he
slipped the noose over his head and adjusted it to his neck. .
. . Colonel Scammell now informed him that he had an opportunity to speak, if he desired it. He raised the handker-
chief from his eyes and said: 'I pray you to bear me witness
that I meet my fate like a brave man. 17.

One of the soldiers provided a graphic description of the final moments:

He was dressed in what I would call a complete British uniform; coat of the brightest scarlet, faced or trimmed with the
most beautiful green. His vest and breeches were bright buff.
. . . He had a long and beautiful head of hair, which, agreeably
to the fashion, was wound with a black ribbon and hung down
his back. All eyes were upon him; and it is not believed that
any other officer of the British army, placed in this situation,
would have appeared better than this unfortunate man. . . .

The wagon was then very suddenly drawn from under the

gallows; which, together with the length of the rope gave him a most tremendous swing but in a few minutes he hung entirely still. He remained hanging twenty or thirty minutes, and during that time the chambers of death were never stiller than the multitude by which he was surrounded. Orders were given to cut the rope and take him down without letting him fall. [When I could get close] I saw his uniform was taken off and the body laid in the coffin. It was indeed a shocking sight. . . . 19.

Thus, John Andre became the only person who paid for Benedict Arnold's treachery with his life. Andre's nobility in accepting his death contrasted sharply with people's reactions to Benedict Arnold.

## Hostile Responses

Both Benedict Arnold and General Clinton had been convinced that tens of thousands of Americans would follow Arnold's lead by switching sides and that would bring the American Revolution to a quick end. They could not have been more wrong. The reaction against Arnold was swift and overwhelming. His military career was instantly reinterpreted, and many of his most heroic acts were disregarded. Adjutant General Alexander Scammel said that Arnold's "conduct and sufferings . . . has in the eyes of the Army and his country covered a series of base, groveling, dirty, scandalous and rascally peculation and fraud; and the Army and the country [ever] indulgent and partial to an officer who has suffered in the common cause, wished to cover his faults, and we were even afraid to examine too closely, for fear of discovering some of his rascality." 20. Mad Anthony Wayne was even more outspoken and insisted that "Arnold never possessed either fortitude or personal bravery—he was naturally a coward and never went in the way of danger but stimulated by liquor even to intoxication." 21.

General Washington noted the contrast between the brave heroism of Andre and the treachery of Arnold. "Andre has met his fate, and with that fortitude which was to be expected from an accomplished man, and gallant officer.

But I am mistaken if at *this time*, Arnold is undergoing the torments of a mental Hell. He wants feeling! From some traits of his character which have lately come to my knowledge, he seems to have been so hackneyed in villainy, and to be so lost to all sense of honor and shame that while his faculties will enable him to continue his sordid pursuits, there will be no time for remorse." 22.

In Philadelphia, Boston, and scores of smaller towns, people burned or hanged Arnold in life-sized effigy. He was shown seated, given two faces, with the devil standing behind him, shaking a purse at Arnold's left ear, while in his other hand was a pitchfork raised to drive Arnold into hell as a reward for his crimes. After being dragged through the streets, the effigy was hanged and then burned. Reaction was particularly vicious in his home state of Connecticut, where effigies were given humiliating treatment. In Norwich, mobs invaded a cemetery and destroyed every tombstone containing the hated name of *Arnold*, including that of his father.

Benedict's childhood was quickly reinvented to include countless tales demonstrating that he was in the clutches of the Devil from the earliest age. Rhymes and songs were used by parents to warn children of behaving like Benedict.

Throughout the rest of 1780 and 1781, a wave of patriotic fervor swept the country.

As soon as he fled West Point, Arnold sought ways to justify or explain his treasonous acts. He was not above using threats to make others appear in the wrong. In a letter to Washington, for example, received by the commander less than two hours after Andre's death, Arnold argued that Andre should not be blamed for decisions made by Arnold. But, if Andre should be held responsible, "I shall think myself bound by every tie of duty and honor to retaliate on such unhappy persons in your army as may fall within my power. . . . If this warning should be disregarded, and he suffer, I call Heaven and earth to witness, that your Excellency will be justly answerable for the torrent of blood that may be spilt in consequence." 23.

Throughout his life, Benedict insisted that he was in the right. Thus, he felt quite justified in threatening Washington. In a similar way, he knew how deeply Clinton was pained by the death of Andre, but he waited only a few days before pressing him to settle how much the British were going to pay him for his treason. Clinton was understandably annoyed at being dunned by his co-conspirator, but he paid Arnold handsomely within the next two weeks.

Benedict received just about everything he could have hoped for. In fact, no American officer made as much money during the war as he did. The initial sum Clinton had commissioned was 6,000 pounds plus 315 pounds—the 6,315 total being equivalent to between $60,000 and $80,000 in today's purchasing power. That was just the beginning. Arnold also received pay of 450 pounds a year as a cavalry officer, reduced to half for life after the war.

There were other sources of income: In March 1782, the King issued a warrant to his paymaster of pensions that "Our will and pleasure is, and we do hereby direct, authorize and command, that an annuity or yearly pension of five hundred pounds be established and paid to you unto Margaret Arnold, wife of our trusty and well beloved brigadier general, Benedict Arnold." As Van Doren discovered in Clinton's papers, Sir Henry had noted in regard to the pension that she had performed "services which [were] very meritorious." 25. In addition, each of Arnold's five surviving children with Peggy received annual pensions of 100 pounds. His three sons by Margaret Mansfield were rewarded with British army commissions: Benedict in 1780 at age twelve, Richard and Henry a year later when they were twelve and nine respectively. The total pensions paid to the family each year totaled 1,450 pounds, or about $20,000 in modern purchasing power. Finally, in 1798, the Arnolds received 13,400 acres of Canadian lands set aside for Loyalists.

Benedict may have done well in financial terms, but he had to be displeased with the negative reaction of the British army and people in New York. The British officers had been extremely fond of Major Andre and his execution was a shock; they could not help but associate Arnold's escape with Andre's death. Nearly all of the officers vowed not to serve under the turncoat.

In an effort to justify his actions and to persuade dissatisfied Patriots to join him, Arnold wrote two addresses to the American people. He was aided by Judge William Smith, a leading Loyalist. The first, "To the Inhabitants of America," was printed on October 25. In his address to the American people, he tried to argue that he was never a believer in the Declaration of Independence—although during his 1780 court-martial, he said he thought the declaration was "glorious." He also said that Great Britain's 1778 Act of Reconciliation gave Americans everything they had asked for, short of independence. That, combined with his belief that the French planned to take over when the British left, convinced him it was better to return to British rule. To the officers and soldiers of the army, he offered a bonus and good salaries for all who would join him in his body of cavalry and infantry. He said he wanted a chosen band of Americans to "share in the glory of rescuing our native country from the grasping hand of France as well as from the ambitious and interested views of a desperate party among ourselves . . . who have brought the colonies to the very brink of destruction." 26.

In the same month, Benedict also wrote to Lord George Germain outlining "The Present strength of the American Rebel Army, Navy, and France." After showing the weaknesses and resignations of the armies and navy, he assured Germain that with a few bribes he could quickly raise a force of up to three thousand former rebels to fight with a large British force, in which he hoped to serve as a major general.

All Arnold's efforts at persuasion had few positive results. Fewer than 100 Rebels chose to change sides. And he did not count on the negative reactions of the British officers, or the unwillingness of Clinton to make him a major general or to let him command a major attack on one of Washington's armies. Clinton did, however, encourage his new colonel to form his American Legion—a force of about 1,700 men, half of them British regulars and Hessians, the rest, Loyalists. Benedict set to work for the British with as much energy and skill as he had formerly used against them.

## The Kidnap Attempt

While Colonel Arnold was planning a raid on Virginia, General Washington approved a plan to kidnap the traitor. The plan was the brainchild of Major "Light Horse Henry" Lee. Washington insisted that Arnold be captured alive; the commander wanted to make an example of him. Lee centered his plan around Sergeant John Champe, a powerful and ambitious member of Lee's cavalry.

The plan called for Champe to desert on October 20, and once approved by the British, join Arnold's Legion, and work his way close to Arnold. Champe played his part perfectly and carried out an exciting cloak-and-dagger scheme.

Champe studied Arnold's movements and planned, with accomplices, to seize him during his habitual midnight stroll in his garden. They would bind and gag Arnold and carry him into an adjoining alley, and from there to the Hudson River where another accomplice was waiting with a boat. If they were stopped they would say that Arnold was a soldier drunk on duty whom they were taking to the guardhouse. Once they were safely in the boat they would row across the Hudson where Lee would be waiting with a squadron of dragoons.

As so often happened in schemes involving Arnold, however, totally unforeseen circumstances changed everything. On the very day of the planned kidnapping, Champe's unit was ordered to board its transports. Lee waited nervously all night with no idea what had happened. Champe ended up serving under Arnold in Virginia for five months before he had a chance to escape back to the Americans. It is unlikely that Arnold ever knew how close he came to feeling Washington's revenge.

# Chapter Thirteen

## The Mystery of Peggy Shippen Arnold

Peggy Shippen Arnold was one of the most fascinating women of her time. Even in her late teens, she was known for her beauty and charm. Educated at home in the traditional subjects of music, art, literature, and household arts, she also received special training from her father that enabled her to converse intelligently on a variety of topics, including business and politics. All these qualities combined to produce a magnetism that kept men of all ages captivated, even years after her marriage to Benedict Arnold.

During her lifetime and in the years since, there have been countless questions about her role in Arnold's treason. This chapter reviews the evidence and opinions that have emerged over the 250 years since the betrayal. The weight of the evidence, much of it circumstantial, will show how deep her involvement was.

### Early Opinions

Many of Peggy's contemporaries were certain that she was totally incapable of being part of a conspiracy. A half-century later, historians were still convinced that this

> flighty young woman would [never] be trusted with secrets by
> her husband or anyone else. . . . Perhaps a different wife would
> have kept the general on the straight and narrow. [He] had no
> counselor on his pillow to urge him to follow the rugged path
> of a Revolutionary patriot. 1.

The discoveries of Carl Van Doren in the 1930s began to change ideas about Peggy's role. He revealed, for example, that within two weeks of her marriage to Benedict in April, 1779, he made his first secret overture to the

British through shopkeeper Joseph Stansbury, who became the trusted go-between with British Major John Andre. It seems quite certain that the couple would at least discuss the matter before Benedict made the fatal move. Even with Van Doren's new evidence, however, later biographers concluded that Peggy's role was "a very controversial one." 2. As recently as 1997, biographer James Kirby Martin wrote that "historians have not resolved the extent of her involvement in her husband's perfidy, although Peggy certainly knew about his contacts with Andre." 3.

Although uncertainty about Peggy's involvement has continued, evidence of a partnership with her husband keeps piling up. For example, in Major Andre's first letter to Benedict, in which he explained the code system they would be using, he added that he wanted Peggy involved in the exchange of messages: "The Lady might write to me at the same time with one of her intimates—she will guess who I mean—the latter remaining ignorant of interlining, [and Peggy] will send the letter. . . . The letters may talk of the Meschianza and other nonsense." 4. In other words, Peggy would receive a letter from her friend, then write a secret message to Andre between the lines in invisible ink. The friend was Peggy Chew, who was Peggy's best friend and had acted in the Meschianza for Andre.

Arnold replied in his first coded letter: "Madam Arnold presents you her particular compliments." The conclusion seems unavoidable: Peggy was deeply involved from the very beginning, including her own secret message to Andre, which may not have been read by Benedict in every case.

### Other Evidence of Peggy's Early Involvement

In late 1778, New York State made its offer of an estate and land to Arnold as a reward for his heroic actions in the state. Benedict immediately headed north to discuss the possibilities with General Schuyler. Peggy, who had not yet given Arnold her consent to marriage, was not thrilled by the prospect of living in the wilds of New York, where Indian tribes still held sway over large areas.

Benedict never made it to New York. He turned back largely because the

Pennsylvania Council filed eight criminal charges against him, charges that would be tried by court-martial. Timing became a factor at this point. When Arnold brought up the possibility of purchasing the handsome Mount Pleasant Estate a few miles outside of Philadelphia, Peggy's attitude changed completely; in fact, her wedding to Benedict took place barely two weeks after the purchase was made. It probably helped, too, that Arnold deeded the estate to Peggy and himself—plus her heirs—for life. Some writers have concluded that the purchase of Mount Pleasant was crucial in persuading Peggy's father to grant his permission for the marriage. Edward Shippen, however, had said that the decision was Peggy's to make; he did not have to grant permission.

The New York offer could have been perfect for Benedict. He might have escaped the clutches of Joseph Reed and his Pennsylvania Council. The estate and the possible sale of some 40,000 acres could have given his finances a big boost. Instead, he added a huge sum to his indebtedness with the purchase of Mount Pleasant. One is tempted to conclude that Peggy made good use of Benedict's desire for her to maneuver him toward the decision she wanted. Several authors have mentioned her strong romantic hold over him. For example, Willard Wallace wrote: "Demure and innocent before marriage, she soon evinced a capacity for passion that enthralled the vigorous Arnold." 5. There were surprising elements of her personality that have often been overlooked; for example, there was a sensuality about her that apparently was not shared by her two older sisters or many of her other contemporaries. As Wallace commented: "Perhaps it would have been remarkable if, with her background and her many Loyalist and British friends, she had not encouraged her discontented fiancé to take the decisive step that would bring him both revenge and vindication." 6.

In a letter to Peggy on February 8, 1779, he seems to indicate that he was happily giving up New York's offer. "Heavens!" he exclaimed, "what I must have suffered had I continued my journey—the loss of happiness for a few dirty acres. I can almost bless the villainous roads and more villainous men who oblige me to return." 7.

Another circumstance that points to Peggy's influence involves Benedict's first step in offering his services to General Clinton. How did Arnold know that Joseph Stansbury was a man who could be trusted with messages requiring the greatest secrecy? There is little doubt that he learned about the man from Peggy; she, in turn, was most likely introduced to him by Andre. Since Stansbury had performed charity work for Clinton, he might have attended social functions with Andre and Peggy.

Additional evidence pointing to Peggy's early involvement in the conspiracy has to do with the key plan of gaining control of West Point, then selling it to the British for a large sum. Modern authors have insisted that West Point was never mentioned before the late summer of 1780. However, Shippen family papers indicate that Peggy said she suggested the West Point scheme in May of 1779. Scholars insist that these statements are merely hearsay, since Peggy's letter(s) have not been found. 8.

In support of the Shippen family's contention, Andre wrote two months later in a coded suggestion to Benedict: "Permit me to prescribe a little exertion. It is the procuring of an accurate plan of West Point." 9. Another year would pass before Arnold would persuade Washington to give him command of West Point. By that time, all the conspirators were convinced that the complex of forts was the crucial piece in their scheme to bring the American Revolution to a speedy end.

### Peggy and John Andre

During the British occupation of Philadelphia, Peggy had enjoyed a close relationship with British Captain John Andre, General Howe's aide de camp. Andre's charm and talents added liveliness to Howe's headquarters. In addition to his cheerfulness and skills, he wrote poetry and plays, designed scenery and costumes, and also acted and directed. He created an extravagant production as a special farewell to General Howe, who was being replaced by General Clinton. The colorful production, called the *Mischianza*, featured Turkish-style pantalooned costumes, including one that Andre designed for Peggy, which was so revealing that her father forbade her to wear it. Peggy was not used to being denied by her father or anyone else, but she chose not to attend the event, out of deference to him.

Peggy clearly enjoyed the months of British occupation of Philadelphia, especially the attentions of Andre and his fellow officers. Andre was a frequent visitor to the Shippen home. He escorted seventeen-year-old Peggy to social functions several times a week, sometimes with her two older sisters. He continued to write to her after the British left Philadelphia for New York. When Clinton replaced Howe, he retained Andre, promoted him to major, and made him his adjutant general, a position at which he showed great skill, especially in intelligence matters.

How close was Peggy's relationship with Andre? Van Doren, who made extensive use of British War Office records, concluded: "There is only the slightest foundation for the romantic story that Andre had been in love with Peggy Shippen, or she with him." 10. But there is an interesting circumstance supporting the idea of a love affair: Writing nearly a century after Peggy's death in 1804, her grandson Colonel Pownell Phipps wrote, "Poor Andre was in love with her, but she refused him for Arnold. [After her death] we found a locket with a lock of Andre's hair which we still have." 11. Keeping that lock of his hair for the last 35 years of her life suggests something more than a friendship. As far as Peggy's family was concerned, then, there seems to have been little or no question about how close she and Andre had been.

Whatever their relationship had been, it seems certain that, once she committed herself to Benedict, that commitment was deep and lifelong. In fact, they seem to have been completely devoted to each other. There appears to be no evidence to support the notion that behind her powerful efforts to make the West Point scheme work was a secret desire to be reunited with Andre in New York.

### The Theatrics of Peggy Arnold

One of the difficulties in analyzing how deeply Peggy Arnold was involved in Benedict Arnold's treason is the confusion that Peggy herself thrust into the issue. From the moment Arnold's treason was exposed with the arrival of General Washington and the news of Andre's arrest, Peggy Arnold was never under suspicion. Washington did feel that those closest to Benedict—his two aides, Varick and Franks—and Peggy had to be interviewed for any information they might have.

After Arnold stumped upstairs to their bedroom to tell her the stunning news of Andre's arrest with the telltale documents, Peggy knew she had very little time to prepare for the questions that were sure to come. Washington arrived about thirty minutes after Arnold made his escape and was being rowed to the *Vulture*. All was quiet from Peggy's room until Washington and his aides left for the Point, thinking to meet Arnold there.

Peggy apparently started to go downstairs to Colonel Varick's room, where he was lying ill, as he had been the day before when she brought him tea. Varick, who was terribly fond of her, suddenly heard her scream for him from the top of the stairs. He instantly rushed up to her, and this is how he described the scene:

> With her hair disheveled and flowing about her neck, a morning gown with few other clothes remained on her—too few to be seen even by the gentlemen of the family, much less by many strangers. . . . She seized me by the hand with this—to me—distressing address and a wild look: 'Colonel Varick, have you ordered my child to be killed?' Judge you my feelings at such a question from this most amiable and distressed of her sex, whom I most valued. She fell on her knees at my feet with prayers and entreaties to spare her innocent babe. . . . I attempted to raise her up, but in vain. Major Franks and Dr. Eustis soon arrived, and we carried her to her bed, raving mad. 12.

For a time, she was quiet, Varick continued, then "she burst again into pitiable tears and exclaimed to me—alone on her bed with her—that she had not a friend left here." He tried to assure her that she had him and Franks, and that Arnold would soon return with General Washington.

"'No, General Arnold will never return!' she cried, sobbing and gesturing toward the ceiling. 'He is gone, he is gone forever; there, there, there! The spirits have carried him up there.'" 13.

Later, after dinner, Washington had a chance to walk in the garden and talk first with Franks, then with Varick. He assured them both that they were not under suspicion but he was anxious to hear what they knew of Arnold's movements in recent weeks.

When Peggy asked to see Washington, he agreed. She told Varick that there was a red-hot iron on her head and only the General could remove it. But when Washington entered her room, she exclaimed: "No, that is not General Washington! That is the man who was a-going to assist Colonel Varick in killing my child." 14. Without saying more, Washington quietly left the room. He had known Peggy most of her life and had always been fond of her, so this encounter must have been hard for him. Lafayette, who was deeply sympathetic to Peggy, remarked, "She looked on us all as murderers." 15.

The next morning, Lafayette and Hamilton visited her room to try to comfort her. In a letter to his fiancé Betsy Schuyler (General Schuyler's daughter), Hamilton wrote:

> She received us in bed with every circumstance that would interest our sympathy, and her sufferings were so eloquent that I wished myself her brother to be her defender. . . . Could I forgive Arnold for sacrificing his honor, reputation, and duty, I could not forgive him for acting a part that must have forfeited the esteem of so fine a woman. 16.

Historians George F. Scheer and Hugh F. Rankin speculated that Betsy Schuyler must have noticed "Peggy's cleverness in setting the scene [on her bed and still wearing very little]." 17. Was Peggy play-acting through all these histrionics? Few writers are willing to go that far. As Willard Wallace put it: "Whether she was play-acting at West Point cannot be determined for a certainty." 18.

A major reason for questioning Peggy's acting ability is the evidence of an earlier incidence of hysteria: Shortly before Peggy left Philadelphia for West Point, she dined at the home of Robert Morris. A friend of the Arnolds, arriving late, congratulated her on Benedict being appointed to a command far more prestigious than West Point. This was a reference to the mistaken announcement that Arnold had been named to command the left wing of the army.

Morris reported that Peggy immediately went into "hysteric fits. Efforts were made to convince her that the general had been chosen for a preferable station. These explanations, however, to the astonishment of all present, produced no effect." 19.

Many writers have concluded that the incident proves that Peggy was given to hysterics and her fits at West Point were merely an extension of that response. But that interpretation ignores how much was at stake for her. Months of planning and scheming had come to depend completely on Arnold being in command at West Point. Without that, their dream was shattered. It seems quite likely, then, that her hysterical fit at the Morris home was a genuine reaction to a great shock.

At West Point, on the other hand, Peggy knew that everything depended on her being in control of every situation. If her West Point hysterics were genuine, they were very effective. If she was acting, which seems probable, it worked perfectly.

Peggy could not have hand-picked a better audience for her acting at West Point. Hamilton, Lafayette, Varick, and Franks were all young—under thirty—vigorous men of action, who had spent most of the past four years living in military camps and waging war. And, as Washington had said, all the young men were already in love with her.

Twenty-three-year-old Alexander Hamilton tried to explain Peggy's appeal to his fiancé: When they went to her in the morning, he wrote, "she was still frantic with distress. . . . It was the most affecting scene I was ever witness to. One moment she raved, another she melted into tears. Sometimes she pressed her infant to her bosom and lamented its fate . . . in a manner that would have pierced insensitivity itself. . . . All the sweetness of beauty, all the loveliness of innocence, all the tenderness of a wife, and all the fondness of a mother showed themselves in her appearance and conduct. We have every reason to believe that she was entirely unacquainted with the plan." 20. Washington was no youngster, of course, but he did have a soft spot for the ladies, and he seems to have been as convinced by Peggy's theatrical display as the younger men had been.

The next day, Washington gave her the choice of going to her husband in

New York or to her family in Philadelphia. She chose to go to her family, and late in the day, she was on her way, with Major Franks as her escort. Her hysterics had apparently subsided.

## Enter Aaron Burr

On the ride to Philadelphia, Peggy and Major Franks made several overnight stops. One was at the home of Mrs. Theodosia Prevost, said to be the wife of a British officer, but who two years later married Aaron Burr. This stop led to unusual testimony about Peggy and her role in the treason.

According to Burr, when strangers were present, Peggy had fits of sobbing. But when she was alone with Theodosia, Burr said, "Mrs. Arnold became tranquillized, and assured Mrs. Prevost that she was heartily sick of the theatrics. . . ," She also spoke of her role in the conspiracy: "She stated that she had corresponded with the British commander [Clinton]—that she was disgusted with the American cause and those who had the management of public affairs—and that through great persuasion and unceasing perseverance, she had ultimately brought General Arnold into an arrangement to surrender West Point to the British." 21.

Burr's story is intriguing, but there are several problems with it. First, there is Burr himself. Many question his reliability, since his career is marked by countless self-serving statements, often of questionable veracity. He later became nearly as notorious as Arnold, when as vice president, he killed Hamilton in a duel, then fled west where he hooked up with another unusual figure—James Wilkinson—in a scheme that might have involved establishing an empire west of the Mississippi. That blew up when Wilkinson turned him in.

In the Prevost incident, the story did not come to light until after both Arnold and Peggy were dead. This delay was said to have stemmed from Burr's basic decency. The Shippen family denied any decency on Burr's part. Relying on family letters, they claimed that Burr had become Peggy's escort for part of the journey to Philadelphia:

> On the way he made love to this afflicted lady, thinking to take advantage of her just feelings of indignation toward her husband, to help him in his infamous design. Yet this is the

fact; if our tradition be true. And indignantly repelled, he treasured up his revenge, and left a story behind him worthy of his false and malignant heart. . . ." 22.

There is an unusual addition to this already unusual Aaron Burr story: Benedict Arnold, in his *Memoirs*, written in the 1790s, stated that Peggy told him about her encounter with Burr as soon as she was reunited with him in New York in November, 1780. According to the diary, when Peggy and her escort reached Paramus, Major Franks turned her over to Aaron Burr, to escort her the rest of the way to Philadelphia. The *Memoirs* account continues:

Aaron Burr [was] a friend of her childhood, under whose escort as an American officer, she was to proceed. Neither capacity prevented his endeavoring to seduce her on the way, and
then, on being repulsed, circulating that she was party to my
'treason,' and that all her hysterics before Washington . . . had
been but acting, and that she had confided to Mrs. Prevost
that she was tired of 'playing a part.'

That Burr had the audacity to attempt the seduction of my wife
in the very house of the woman he afterward married, and then
call her as witness to a scandal he circulated about Peggy suffi-
ciently characterizes both parties [Burr and Theodosia].

But Peggy, frightened, and at a loss for a friend . . . had unwill-
ingly to accept Burr's protection for the rest of the journey,
and only when safe in the arms of her father did she tell of
Burr's insult and her rebuff. The father dared not challenge,
and I [after] Peggy told me, could not. 23.

This entry in Arnold's *Memoirs* seems to confirm Aaron Burr's account, including the contention that Peggy was a major player in the treasonous scheme,
and that it was her "persuasion" and "perseverance" that persuaded Arnold to
take the fatal step.

The two accounts provide a very tempting "smoking gun" piece of evidence.
However, I can't be sure that Benedict's diary is any more reliable than Burr's

account in the Davis biography. Arnold's diary was first published in 1917 by Charles Scribner's Sons. After the book was out of print for many years, a facsimile edition was published in 2010, but with no new editor or copyright. The 620-page facsimile does seem accurate, although the narrative is often self-serving. Consequently I've used it only when it is verified by other sources. In addition, I have not found the 1917 original listed among the sources in any of the books used in preparing the present volume. The result is that I hesitate to present Peggy's encounter with Burr as *proof* of her leading role in Arnold's treason. But the two accounts do add intriguing possibilities to the growing body of evidence.

While Peggy's family was delighted to welcome her to Philadelphia, others were not. Authorities had already searched the Arnold household and one of the letters they discovered was from Andre to Peggy. It was assumed that the letter proved Peggy's complicity in the treason, and the government decided she was no longer welcome in the city. Joseph Reed's Executive Council resolved "that the said Margaret Arnold depart this state within fourteen days from the date hereof, and that she do not return again during the continuance of the present war." 24.

Accompanied most of the way by her father, Peggy went to New York to join her husband, arriving on November 14, 1780. The Shippen family tried every means available to have the ruling changed so she could remain in Philadelphia, but nothing worked. They assumed that Peggy had no desire to go to New York, failing to recognize her total commitment to her husband. (Hannah left Philadelphia at the same time, taking the three boys from Benedict's first marriage to New Haven. She always remained loyal to her brother and later joined him and Peggy in England.)

## The Weight of the Evidence

No modern writers have concluded that Peggy Arnold was at least an equal co-conspirator with her husband. Carl Van Doren in the 1930s went farther than anyone since. He wrote:

> However beguiling she may have been during the warm days
> of courtship & honeymoon, she could hardly have done more

than confirm a powerful will like Arnold's in its own decision. Even if it was actually she who proposed the treachery—and there is no first-hand evidence that she did—the final responsibility must lie with the mature & experienced Arnold for undertaking to carry it out. 24.

If we consider the evidence—and the timing—some interesting conclusions become possible:

First, Peggy's "beguiling" ways were working on a man who was feeling harassed, isolated, and with Washington's reprimand, quite abandoned and defeated. For years his enemies had pounced on him at every opportunity, so that even his great battlefield triumphs became clouded by personal attacks and denial of recognition. During the year of court cases and hearings on finances, Peggy was always there—beautiful, warm, something like the "Beckoning Fair One" of the English short story, loving—but just out of reach during the months before their marriage. He might have become desperate and confused enough to think she was pointing in the right direction.

In the first three months of 1779, events moved him steadily to the frame of mind Peggy hoped he would achieve:

- Late Dec. '78 – Feb. 1779: New York State's generous offer; Benedict's trip aborted by criminal charges. Letter to Peggy—relief that he didn't trade happiness for a "few acres."

- March, 1779: Peggy thrilled by new idea of a Pennsylvania home—Purchase of Mt. Pleasant completed on March 22.

- April 8, '79: Peggy and Benedict are married.

- May, '79: Somewhere during these few weeks, Peggy has quietly urged Benedict to turn to her friends in New York—Loyalists and British officers who could make things easy for him. She provided the name of Joseph Stansbury and how reliable he will be. She might even bring up the idea for West Point as the least bloody way for him to become the peacemaker.

Of course, there is no "first-hand evidence" of her central role in bringing about the betrayal; Peggy was not likely to write her step-by-step plan to persuade him to move in the direction she wanted to go. Aaron Burr's account, supported by Arnold's version, would come close to first-hand evidence, but are these two sources reliable enough?

Later episodes add to the weight of circumstantial evidence. Her hysterics at the Robert Morris house demonstrated how heavily she relied on the West Point scheme. And the acting out of hysterics at West Point illustrated her masterful self control. She left for Philadelphia on September 27th; Arnold had made his escape on the 26th.

Over the next twenty years, as Benedict and Peggy tried to build a new life in England, she displayed some of her remarkable abilities. She managed their finances skillfully and when Benedict's business schemes failed—and later his health also failed—Peggy was always there to prop him up and restore his confidence. After his death in 1801, she performed financial wizardry to pay off all of their considerable debts in a very short time.

## Reunion and Reactions

Benedict was thrilled and relieved when Peggy and Neddy arrived on November 14. He had just rented a handsome town house adjacent to Clinton's headquarters. The weeks since their frantic separation in late September had not been easy for either of them.

Arnold found that his reception in New York was not what he had hoped for. Some people were mildly curious about him, which made them polite, but only Clinton and Judge William Smith acted in friendly ways. But a major problem had been created by the execution of John Andre. People could not help but think that Arnold escaped with his life, while Andre paid with his.

Andre had been tremendously popular with the British army, especially the younger officers. Arnold must have been deeply hurt when he learned that the young officers unanimously refused to serve under him. The arrival of Peggy and their son helped improve the mood. She was well known to many British officers who remembered pleasant visits to the Shippen home. Loyalist and British women, not having been in Philadelphia, were polite but decidedly lukewarm. One Loyalist woman—Mrs. Rebecca Shoemaker—commented that "Peggy Arnold is not so much admired for her beauty as one might have expected. All allow she has great sweetness in her countenance, but wants animation, sprightliness, and that fire in her eyes. . . ." 26.

One area where the Arnolds did well was in the amounts the British were willing to pay for their treason.

## How Treason Paid

Throughout his life, Arnold always insisted that he was in the right. Thus, he felt quite justified in threatening Washington over the trial and execution of John Andre. Similarly, even though he knew how pained Clinton was by Andre's death, Benedict waited only a few days before pressing him about money and rank.

General Clinton was irritated by Arnold's pushiness, but he was also a man of honor and he understood Benedict's need. In a similar way, he had earnestly wished that Washington would not have Andre executed, but he understood why Washington felt he could not counter his court's verdict. The military etiquette of the time also dictated that neither man could approve an exchange of Arnold for Andre. Consequently, Clinton wasted little time in addressing Arnold's needs.

Benedict received just about everything he could have hoped for. In fact, it's likely that no American officer made as much money during the war as he did. The initial sum Clinton had commissioned was 6,000 pounds plus 315 pounds for expenses—the 6,315 total being equivalent to between $60,000 and $80,000 in today's purchasing power. That was just the beginning. Arnold also received pay of 450 pounds a year as a cavalry officer, reduced to half for life after the war. He also received an additional 250 pound salary as a wartime brigadier general.

There were other sources of income. For a time, he was a favorite of King George. In March, 1782, the King issued a warrant to his paymaster of pensions that "our will and pleasure is, and we do hereby direct, authorize and command, that an annuity or yearly pension of five hundred pounds be established and paid to you unto Margaret Arnold, wife of our trusty and well beloved brigadier general, Benedict Arnold.". In addition, each of Arnold's five surviving children with Peggy received annual pensions of 100 pounds, thanks to Queen Catherine's fondness for Peggy. [Peggy bore a second son in New York, then five more in England—three sons and two daughters. One son and a daughter died in infancy.] His three sons by Margaret Mansfield were rewarded with British army commissions: Benedict in 1780 at age twelve, Richard and Henry a year later when they were twelve and nine respectively. The total pensions paid to the family each year totaled 1,450 pounds, or about $20,000 in modern dollars. Finally, in 1798, the Arnolds received 13,400 acres of Canadian lands set aside for Loyalists.

## Efforts to Win Converts

Both Arnold and General Clinton had been confident that tens of thousands of disgruntled Americans would follow Benedict's lead in returning their loyalty to the King. Only a handful chose to become traitors. Instead a wave of patriotism swept the country, coupled with a hatred of the man who had betrayed them.

In desperation, Benedict tried to persuade people to join him. He wrote two essays to the American people and soldiers, explaining his reasons. Loyalist Judge William Smith helped him with ideas and wording.

In the first essay, which was printed in newspapers, he explained his treason as a reaction to the danger posed by France. He also accused Congress of "tyranny . . . and a total disregard of the interest and welfare of the people."

The second essay was addressed to "The soldiers and officers of the Continental Army who have the real Interest of their Country at Heart and who are determined to be no longer the Tools and Dupes of Congress, or of France." In the course of the article, he asked such questions as "What is America but a land of widows, beggars, and orphans?" 27.

Benedict's efforts were remarkably unsuccessful. People's distaste for Arnold's treachery translated into an urgent sense of unity and patriotic fervor, especially in the South. The Continental Army and local militia were eager to fight, in spite of ragged uniforms, and a shortage of food and other supplies.

## Patriot Responses

The Patriots were blessed with outstanding leaders. After the disastrous loss in the August battle of Camden, Congress gave up on Galloping Gates and wisely let Washington name a new general in the South. He selected Nathanael Greene, only 38 years old, but highly regarded by the soldiers and officers.

Greene's first move was a daring one. Although his army was badly outnumbered by the British under Cornwallis, Greene decided to divide his army. Greene led one division in guerilla attacks on Cornwallis. Veteran Daniel Morgan led the other division. Both generals were aided by hit-and-run specialists Francis Marion (the "Swamp Fox") and Thomas Sumter (the "Caroline Gamecock"). Brilliantly orchestrated victories at King's Mountain, in October 1780 and the Cowpens, early 1781 drove the British and Loyalists out of the Carolinas and forced Cornwallis toward the Virginia coast and his eventual trap at Yorktown.

Benedict Arnold pushed ahead in spite of the disappointments. He formed his own American Legion regiment, with the rank of cavalry captain, plus the wartime rank of brigadier general. His regiment, in addition to deserters, included elements of: the 18th Irish regiment (mostly New York Loyalists); Colonel John Simcoe's Loyalist Queen's Rangers (mostly New York deserters); and Captain John Thomas's Bucks County Pennsylvania Volunteers. For his first raid against his former country, he had about 1,700 men. This included a few hundred British regulars, who were probably added by Clinton because he did not entirely trust his turncoat general.

# CHAPTER FOURTEEN

# Nil Desperandum: the Final Years

ARNOLD'S LIFE HAD CONSISTED OF a few flashes of brilliance, first in making money, then in battlefield glory. But each triumph was followed by criticism and a failure to achieve recognition. The disappointments were the product of his own character flaws combined with the attacks of his numerous enemies, who often picked on those personal weaknesses.

## The Impact of Betrayal

The collapse of his treason was his greatest failure, and it cost him everything he had achieved as a leading patriot. The discovery of the plot left him as a minor footnote in the nation's history. Had he succeeded in selling West Point to the British, he would have gained far greater notoriety as a villain.

Writing in his journal at the time, Dr. Thacher declared: "He aimed to plunge a dagger into the bosom of his country." 1. Had he succeeded, the Patriot cause would have been desperate. With the British in control of West Point and the entire Hudson River, New England would have been cut off from the other states, and Washington's army would have been cut off from the French in Rhode Island. Combined with the low morale of the military and the weakness of the Congress, Arnold's treachery could have sounded the death knell of the Revolution.

There were, fortunately, several factors that could have saved the Patriot cause. First, news of Arnold's betrayal seemed to shock Americans into an urgent new unity. Second, new leaders, like Nathanael Greene and Daniel Morgan, stepped forward and led new offensives. And third, General Clinton became more cautious than ever. He had long been paranoid about losing New York and about confronting Washington; this made him unwilling to make a major push out of his New York base. In addition, he continued to distrust Arnold and that lack of trust grew steadily.

## Benedict's American Legion in Action

Benedict urged Clinton to follow his plan for an attack on Philadelphia, but Clinton rejected it. Instead, he ordered Arnold to launch a raid on the Virginia coast to destroy American supply bases and take control of Portsmouth.

In typical Benedict Arnold fashion, he went about the assignment with great energy and skill. By mid-December, 1780, his 1,600-man force was ready to board transports. After a difficult passage the regiment entered the James River. Arnold launched successful raids on Richmond, Portsmouth, and smaller towns. He came close to capturing Governor Thomas Jefferson.

In the spring, Arnold almost became trapped at Portsmouth. Militia units swarmed the region, and Virginia governor Thomas Jefferson offered a reward for Arnold's capture. Washington sent Lafayette with 1,200 Continentals to Virginia, with orders to hang Arnold if they caught him. The commander also sought help from the French fleet.

Even with enemies all around him, Benedict held on at Portsmouth, determined to fight to the end if the American forces attacked. He vowed to take his own life rather than become a prisoner. Instead, Lord Charles Cornwallis, the handsome, popular commander of British troops in the South, moved into Virginia in May, relieving the pressure on Arnold. Clinton then recalled Benedict and his American Legion, and the disappointed turncoat was back in New York in early June.

## The Raid on New London

The summer of 1781 was not a happy time for Benedict, although he came back with a considerable sum of prize money, his share of the plunder from raids in Virginia, making him, one observer commented, "as rich as a nabob." But he did not gain the military victories or fame he had hoped for.

Throughout the summer, Arnold had little luck gaining recruits for his American Legion. He was also increasingly annoyed with Clinton's lack of initiative and even wrote directly to the British war office in London with his ideas for an attack on Philadelphia. This idea fell through because Cornwallis was reluctant to move troops out of Virginia.

In early September, 1781, Clinton sent Arnold on an amphibious raid on New London, Connecticut. The idea was to destroy this base for American privateers and warships, and also to relieve some of the pressure on Cornwallis in Virginia. Neither Clinton nor Arnold was aware that Washington and Rochambeau had already started their race south to trap Cornwallis at Yorktown, while a French fleet planned to hold the British fleet at bay.

Arnold's raid on New London turned into a needless tragedy, one that reinforced people's view of him as a heartless villain. With about 1,700 troops, mostly British and Hessians, Arnold struck quickly, easily taking the town, destroying many of the ships, as well as a number of warehouses and the largest wharf. Two forts—Trumbull and Griswold—guarded the coast. Fort Trumbull's guns faced the coast, so it fell easily when Arnold attacked it from the rear. Other troops were sent to attack Fort Griswold—and that was when Arnold's skillful victory turned into a disaster.

From a hill above Fort Trumbull, Arnold saw that Fort Griswold was well defended. He sent an officer to the attacking force, ordering them not to attack. But the attack had already begun, with some 800 British assaulting the strong fort which had only about 150 defenders. After bitter fighting, the American defenders finally surrendered and threw down their arms. But the British continued firing and bayoneting for some time, killing 88 Americans and wounding 35 more before their officers gained control. Even though Arnold had tried to rescind the order for the attack, he had also ordered it, making him responsible for the massacre.

While the bloodbath was taking place at the fort, there was more horror at New London. After destroying about a dozen ships, Arnold's men were busy plundering and setting fire to shops, stores, and houses. A sudden shift in the wind sent the flames roaring through the town. Much of New London and nearby Groton were reduced to ashes, with more than 150 houses destroyed.

The American people were naturally outraged by the destruction and bloodshed, and just as naturally blamed Arnold. It was widely assumed that he had destroyed the town in a brutal act of revenge.

Benedict returned to New York, and soon realized that his raid would have no effect on the outcome of the war. It could not even relieve pressure on Cornwallis, since Washington and Rochambeau were closing in on the British at Yorktown. In fact, by mid-September—about a week after the New London raid—Washington's American and French armies were ready to lay siege to Cornwallis at Yorktown. As one American officer said, "We have him in a pudding bag now." Within a month, Cornwallis was forced to surrender, giving the United States the final stirring victory that guaranteed independence. The final peace accord did not come for nearly two years.

Arnold had returned to New York too late to travel south to help at Yorktown, but even after the surrender of Cornwallis, he refused to believe the British should give up. He asked Clinton for permission to go to England to present his ideas. Sir Henry agreed, but said Arnold would have to wait until the French fleet left so that a military convoy could be formed.

The convoy was finally organized in December, 1781. The Arnolds had a second child while in New York, so it was decided that Peggy, the two children, and several servants would sail in a private ship for greater comfort than a Man of War could provide. Arnold sailed in the convoy on the same warship as Lord Cornwallis, who had been allowed to return to England on the promise of not returning to the war.

The ships finally sailed on December 15. Winter storms created a rough crossing and Arnold's ship nearly sank. After limping to a port in the West Indies, Benedict completed the voyage on another ship.

## The Search for a Fresh Start

The Arnolds arrived in London not knowing what to expect. The reception was mixed. Members of the Whig opposition party and people who felt kindly toward America were decidedly unfriendly. But what mattered most to Benedict and Peggy was that they were well received at Court and by government leaders.

Lord Germain was respectful and Sir Guy Carleton, his old adversary, was friendly. King George was very kind and asked him to write his views on conditions in America and the prospects for continuing the war. Peggy was greatly admired for her beauty and bearing. The Queen quickly became very fond of her and let the Court ladies know that she wanted them to befriend her. The Queen also directed the 100-pound pension for each of her children. Peggy had a total of five children, a daughter and three sons; another son and daughter died in infancy.

The Arnolds found a house on Portman Square and looked forward to a prosperous future. Benedict was only forty-three years old and Peggy was still in her early twenties; they felt they had a full life ahead of them. Benedict displayed his optimism by changing his family motto. The old motto was "*mihi gloria sursum*"—"Through glory yielded to me," a recognition that divine gifts created the Arnold family position. The new motto was "*nil desperandum*"—"never despair," a reflection of his determination (and ability) to overcome all obstacles.

In spite of the couple's optimistic beginnings in England, Benedict worried about their income. Their combined annual income of about 1,500 pounds was steady, but there was no way to increase it to meet the needs of his growing family. In addition, to Peggy and their four children, he was also responsible for three sons by his first wife as well as his sister Hannah.

Arnold tried several ways to increase their income. He presented a claim to the government for losses he suffered when American governments seized his assets. His claim amounted to about 45,000 pounds, estimated to equal about $3,000,000 in 21st century dollars.

While Benedict waited for the government's decision, he applied for a position with the private army of the East India Company. Within three days, he received an icy rejection from the company director. The director said that while he trusted Benedict, the majority of people did not. "While this is the case," the letter stated, "no power in this country could suddenly place you in the situation you aim at under the East India Company." 2.

In 1785, Arnold gave up his claims for compensation and decided to try his luck in Canada.

## Canadian Interlude

Eager for a fresh start, Arnold bought and equipped a brig, the *Lord Middleton*, and set sail for Canada in October, 1785, leaving Peggy and their children in London. Determined to regain his past success as a merchant, he settled in New Brunswick, a bustling new town settled by thousands of Loyalists after the Revolution.

Over the next two years, Benedict's life followed a familiar pattern. At first, he enjoyed spectacular success. Shiploads of products from the West Indies brought high profits in New Brunswick and surrounding towns. He bought roughly 15,000 acres of land, built warehouses and stores, and was regarded as the most successful businessman in New Brunswick. He asked Hannah to come to Canada with his three sons and he later sailed to England to get Peggy and their children.

During the long winter of 1785-1786, Peggy became upset by the long silences with no letters from Benedict. It may have been during this time that he took a mistress. The affair, the only time that he was unfaithful to Peggy, produced a son named John Sage. The existence of the illegitimate son was not known until his will was read; the identity of the mother has never been known. During these months, Peggy wrote to her father expressing her worries about Benedict and at being "separated from, and anxious for the fate of the best of husbands." 3.

From the West Indies, Arnold sailed to England, then to New Brunswick with Peggy and the children, arriving in July, 1787. With his entire family in Canada, Benedict worked doubly hard to make a success of his far flung business dealings, and Peggy was content enough, giving birth to another son, George, in September, 1787; she also hoped that she could manage a trip to visit her family in Philadelphia.

A life of success and contentment, however, had always eluded Benedict, and his time in Canada was no different. He was not well liked, even by the Loyalists, in New Brunswick, and his reputation suffered further when the economy of New Brunswick and other parts of Canada suffered a recession caused by increased warfare between England and France. Scores of Loyalists had borrowed money from Arnold or owed him for purchases, and suddenly they could not pay him. Benedict's efforts to collect only served to antagonize his debtors. In some cases, he took debtors to court, winning most of the judgments, which did nothing for his popularity. In 1788, he sailed to England with a cargo. While there, days after he took out an insurance policy, his warehouse in New Brunswick burned to the ground, destroying the contents. Rumors spread that he had started the fire himself to collect the insurance money. His partner joined the chorus of accusers, leading Benedict to sue the man for slander. Arnold won the case, but people continued to believe he was guilty, and many began referring to him as the "Traitor."

To escape the growing hostility, Arnold moved to St. John. Peggy was finally able to make her trip to Philadelphia with her infant son. "My pleasure," she wrote, "will not be unaccompanied by pain; as when I leave you I shall probably bid you adieu forever." 4. After spending several months with her family and friends, she rejoined Benedict in St. John in July, 1790.

By this time, Arnold had decided that they should wind up their affairs in Canada and return to England. The move could not be soon enough for Peggy. She hated the hostility and the "succession of disappointments and mortifications in collecting our debts," she wrote to her sister, as she tried "to shake off that gloom that has taken possession of me and for which I have too much cause." 5.

The year 1791 was a time of almost constant frustration, disappointment, and fear. Benedict's arrogance in his efforts to collect debts added to the anger and hatred. The climax came when a mob surrounded their home and burned an effigy of Arnold in front of the house, calling it "Traitor!" The arrival of troops prevented further trouble.

Arnold tried to sell his extensive holdings but with little success. He finally gave power of attorney to two men, and set sail for England with Peggy and their children in early 1792. Two of his sons from his first marriage— Henry, age nineteen, and Richard, twenty-one-- stayed in Canada with Hannah to try to manage his business affairs. The oldest son, Benedict, entered the army to fight the French.

## A Decade of Despair

There were few happy times in the last decade of Benedict Arnold's life. They did have a few close Loyalist friends and they were proud of their youngest children's progress in school. Lord Cornwallis became a family friend and helped his sons advance in their military careers.

For the most part, however, his desperate efforts to achieve success in the military or in business ended in failure and disappointment.

Within weeks of his arrival, Arnold fought a duel with James Maitland, Earl of Lauderdale, for an insult the earl had made in the House of Lords. Arnold fired first and missed, then was ashamed when Lauderdale refused to shoot. The matter was settled when Lauderdale apologized for his remark and Arnold accepted. This gentlemanly response led to widespread praise for Benedict and great relief for Peggy.

Hoping to take advantage of the favorable comments he had received, Arnold tried to gain a military position. Three months of appeals and letters, however, failed to produce results. As the disappointments increased so did his feelings of failure as a provider. Continued efforts to collect on the Canadian debts accomplished little except more costly lawsuits.

Feeling desperate again, he bought a ship and sailed to the West Indies in 1794 to renew his mercantile ventures. He soon ran into trouble and was taken prisoner by the French. Benedict showed a flash of his old bravado by making a daring escape, and eluding French warships in a rowboat to reach the safety of a British squadron.

Now in his mid-fifties, Arnold found that renewed fighting against France in the West Indies gave him a burst of energy. He served as a "gentleman volunteer" for the British commander, Sir Charles Grey, and was widely praised for his contributions. But he was also deeply disappointed when Grey refused to give him a military post.

In the summer of 1795, he returned to England, much to the relief of Peggy. His enterprises continued to do poorly and there were personal losses as well. His oldest son, Benedict, had been captured by the French and served two years in prison. As soon as he was released, he was sent to the West Indies as an artillery officer. England was in the throes of the long warfare against Napoleon and needed all the officers they could muster. Benedict suffered a leg wound, however, and, when he refused amputation, gangrene set in and he died in October, 1795.

The loss of his oldest son was a heavy blow for Arnold. Later, when their favorite son, Edward, went to India under the sponsorship of Lord Cornwallis, both Arnold and Peggy felt the departure almost as deeply as if he had died. And, in fact, they never did see him again.


The last few years of Arnold's life were a time of increasing disappointment, pain, and despair. He continued to try for a military appointment in 1796, 1797, and 1798, but his appeals were repeatedly turned down or ignored. He finally realized, as he confessed to Peggy, that his military dreams were over and the army was denying him even the chance to die a soldier's death.

There were a number of reasons for the lack of interest in Benedict. Much had changed in England in the nearly two decades since his treason. He was hated by most of the opposition Whigs and by the army's officers. The War Office was focused on the war with post-Revolution France under the leadership of Napoleon. In the late 1790s, England was worried about an attack on London, but the generals never considered Arnold as a possible leader of the city's defense.

In 1800, the stress began to take its toll on his health. He suffered from increasingly severe bouts of asthma, which troubled him day and night, making sleep almost impossible. One leg became badly swollen, probably with gout, and the pain in his wounded leg was now severe, making it difficult for him to stand or walk, even with a cane. Arnold's once powerful physique was also declining, and he became stooped with sagging shoulders and flabby skin.

Peggy was also ill, a semi-invalid with symptoms that were probably the beginning of the cancer that was to take her life in 1804. Through all the suffering, as well as business losses, she continued to support Benedict and keep him propped up. Peggy felt deeply for his misery. Early in 1801, she wrote to

Edward, "He is, at present, in the most harassed wretched state that I have ever seen him. Disappointed in his highly raised expectations, . . . and wishing still to do something, without the health or power of acting, he knows not which way to turn himself." 6.

Throughout Arnold's frenzied last years, a few others expressed sympathy for him. At the end of the Arnolds' stay in Canada, for example, Captain John Shackford had a chance to observe Benedict, who did not remember him from their previous association twenty years earlier. Shackford had been on the Quebec march and had been taken prisoner during the assault on the city. He wrote about seeing Arnold:

> I did not make myself known to him, but frequently . . . I sat upon the ship's deck, and watched the movement of my old commander, who had carried us through everything, and for whose skill and courage I retained my former admiration, despite his treason. But when I thought of what he had been and the despised man he [had become], tears would come, and I could not help it. 7.

Several years later, the French diplomat Charles Maurice de Talleyrand was staying at an inn on the English coast where, he learned, an American general was also staying. Talleyrand introduced himself and, during a rather strained conversation, asked the American if he could supply letters of introduction to his friends in America. Talleyrand recalled:

> He replied,"No," and after a few moments of silence, noticing my surprise, he added, "I am perhaps the only American who cannot give you letters for his own country . . . all the relations I had there are now broken . . . I must never return to the States." He dared not tell me his name. It was General Arnold. I must confess that I felt much pity for him, for which political puritans will perhaps blame me, but with which I do not reproach myself for I witnessed his agony. 8.

The testimony of Talleyrand, Shackford, and Peggy suggest that Arnold was painfully aware of how much he had lost. He could never set foot in his home country and, even after a fairly promising beginning, he did not feel welcome in his adopted country. Continued financial losses pushed him deeper into debt and depression, adding to the awareness of how much property and other assets he had left behind.

By January, 1801, as his symptoms worsened, Benedict seemed to lose the will to live. Desperate to provide for his family, his once sharp business skills were replaced by serious mistakes; sea captains he hired for his last privateers cheated him out of as much as 50,000 pounds. As Peggy commented, "There seems to be a cruel fatality attending all his exertions." 9.

In early June, he experienced several days of extreme agony and occasional delirium, then died "without a groan" on June 14, 1801, in their London home. He was sixty years old.

## Peggy Carries On

Newspapers, both in England and America, paid scant attention to Arnold's passing—most providing only a sentence or two. The *European Magazine* reported that "Benedict Arnold had been a person much noticed during the American War." 10.

In the three years following his death, Peggy displayed her extraordinary devotion plus surprising business acumen. She wrote in careful detail to the children, including her stepsons Richard and Henry in Canada, as well as Hannah, describing his death and his love for all of them. Within a few weeks, she followed up with copies of his will and details of the serious debts he had left. In one letter, written at the end of July, she wrote "that there is but little probability of anything being saved to the family out of this wreck. I fear not even the Furniture, as the debts amount to upwards of 5,000 pounds." With determination, energy, and skill, the young widow, barely in her forties, sold off assets, and lived on a tight budget until she could write, in January, 1804, "I have paid Debts to the Amount of 6,000 pounds; . . . to accomplish this, I have been obliged to make a Sacrifice of many articles of comfort which I had ever considered my own. I sold my Furniture, Wine, Etc., and have not reserved even a towel or a tea spoon, that I have not paid for. . . ." 11. She even managed to set aside a sum for the use of "the best Children in the world," if needed.

Through the more than two years required for these tasks, Peggy suffered incredible internal pain, as the cancer destroyed her system. In a January 1804 letter to Edward she commented simply, "My health is but indifferent." She died August 24, 1804, at the age of forty four.

# *Epilogue*

IN THE BEAUTIFUL ROLLING HILLS OF SARATOGA National Battlefield Park an unusual monument draws visitors' attention. Carved in Vermont granite, it depicts a cavalry officer's boot strapped to a cannon barrel. On the reverse side, the inscription reads:

In Memory of
the "most brilliant soldier" of the
Continental Army, who was desperately wounded
on this spot, the sally port of
BURGOYNE'S "GREAT (WESTERN) REDOUBT"
7th October 1777,
winning for his countrymen
the Decisive Battle of the
American Revolution
and for himself the rank of
Major General

The monument, erected in 1887 by Civil War General John Watts de Peyster, includes de Peyster's name, but not the name of the "most brilliant soldier."

At the time of the momentous victory at Saratoga, the soldiers who won it would have been most pleased to see that monument on the battlefield with Major General Benedict Arnold's name featured in large letters. [de Peyster missed the fact that Arnold was already a major general in October, 1777.]

Throughout his career, no battlefield leader produced more excitement and loyalty than Arnold. After the treason, of course, America's greatest hero became the vilest of villains. In fact, General Nathanael Greene and other Patriots equated his fall with that of Lucifer as the ultimate fall from grace.

Even after that fall, however, many of his former troops could not forget how special he had been. One of those veterans, Private Samuel Downing, summed him up this way:

Arnold was a fighting general, and a bloody fellow he was. He didn't care for nothing, he'd ride right in. It was 'Come on boys!' Twasn't 'Go on, boys!' He was a stern looking man but kind to his soldiers. He was as brave a man as ever lived! They didn't treat him right, but he ought to have been true. 1.

There is no way to excuse or forgive Arnold's teachery. No one made the decision for him and he fully deserves being consigned to the Hell reserved for those who betray their country and its ideals.

There remains, however, a feeling of tragedy about his story. The tragedy comes about because of Peggy and the deep passion they shared. The two seemed to go into their treasonous scheme with their eyes wide open. The trouble was that the vision of each was fatally clouded.

Benedict's vision was distorted by his all-consuming love for Peggy, combined with his desire to avenge the humiliations he had suffered over the previous months and years.

Peggy was a more than willing co-conspirator. She appeared to have a romantic image of her role in helping to heal her brooding, broad-shouldered, deeply wounded lover. The war for her was as a 17-year-old fawned over by young British officers, an enemy personified by handsome Captain John Andre, who was also in love with her. Peggy was sure that she had the charms and skills to strike a deal with those men.

In the comfort and warmth of each other's arms, then, everything seemed possible, and Peggy made it seem easy. She even provided the safe messenger and the idea of making West Point the prize.

The failure of their plan cost them dearly. They spent much of their final twenty years in increasing pain and disappointment. Nothing they tried ever seemed to work out. But they still had each other. Although Peggy destroyed most of Benedict's letters, and her family burned most of hers, neither one was heard to complain about their fate. Peggy did go through a long period of anxiety and depression during and after Arnold's capture by the French in the West

Indies, when she didn't know where he was, or even if he was alive. But they kept trying, and supporting each other, until their time ran out.

The tragic flaw in Benedict Arnold—the traitor within—was his willingness to risk everything in one bold act that would achieve fame, wealth, honor—everything he had always wanted. And key to this desperate undertaking was the partnership with the most beautiful, desirable, and intelligent woman in the world.

# BIBLIOGRAPHY

Abbott, William. *The Crisis of the Revolution: Being the Story of Arnold and Andre.* (1899) reprinted Harbor Hill Books, 1976.

Andre, John. *Major Andre's Journal,* Tarrytown, NY: Wm. Abbott, 1930. Reprinted by New York Times and Arno Press, 1967.

Arnold, Benedict. *Diary/My Story: Being the memoirs of Benedict Arnold: The Late Major-General in the Continental Army and Brigadier-General in That of His Britannic Majesty.* New York: Charles Scribner's Sons, 1917.

Brandt, Clare. *The Man in the Mirror: A Life of Benedict Arnold.* New York: Random House, 1994.

Chernow, Ron. *Washington: A Life.* New York: Penguin Press, 2010.

Davis, M.L. *Memoirs of Aaron Burr.* New York, 1855, 2 vols., reprinted by New York Times and Arno Press, 1967.

Dell, Pamela. *Benedict Arnold: From Patriot to Traitor.* Minneapolis, MN: Compass Point Books, 2005.

Fitzpatrick, J.C. & Sparks: *Writings of George Washington.* Washington, D.C.: 26 vols. 1931-1938. vols. II-VI, XVIII, XX.

Fort Ticonderoga Museum. *The American Champlain Fleet, 1775-1777.* Ticonderoga, Bulletin of the Fort Ticonderoga Museum, vol. 12, no. 14, Sept., 1968.

Gould, Dudley C. *Benedict Arnold.* Middletown, CT: South Farm Press, 2006.

Ketchum, Richard M. *Saratoga: Turning Point of America's Revolutionary War.* New York: Henry Holt Co., 1997.

King, David C. *The United States and Its People.* Menlo Park, CA: Addison-Wesley Publishing Co., 1993.

Martin, James Kirby. *Benedict Arnold, Revolutionary Hero; An American Warrior Reconsidered.* New York: New York University Press, 1997.

Middlekauff, Robert. *The Glorious Cause: The American Revolution, 1763-1789.* New York: Oxford University Press, 1932, 2005.

Murphy, Jim. *The Real Benedict Arnold.* New York, NY: Clarion Books/ Houghton Mifflin, 2007.

Palmer, Dave R. *George Washington and Benedict Arnold: A Tale of Two Patriots.* Washington, DC: Regency Press, 2006.

Purcell, L. Edward & David F. Burg. *The World Almanac of the American Revolution*. New York: World Almanac, 1992.

Raphael, Ray. "America's Disastrous Invasion of Canada". *American History*, Feb. 2010.

Riedesel, Baroness Friederike von. *Letters and Journals Relating to the War of the American Revolution*, 2 vols. Albany: Joel Munsell. Reprinted by the New York Times and Arno Press, 1968.

Roberts, Cokie. *Founding Mothers: The Women Who Raised Our Nation*. New York: Harper Collins/Perennial, 2005.

Roberts, Kenneth. *March to Quebec: Journal of the Members of the Arnold Expedition*. Garden City, NY: Doubleday & Doran, 1938.

Scheer, George F. & Hugh F. Rankin. *Rebels and Redcoats: The American Revolution Through the Eyes of Those Who Fought It and Lived It*. New York: Da Capo Press, Inc. 1957.

Taylor, J.G. *Some New Light on the Later Life and Last Resting Place of Benedict Arnold And his Wife Margaret Shippen*. London: George White, 1931.

Thacher, James. *Military Journal of the American Revolution*. Hartford, 1862. Reprinted by New York Times and Arno Press, 1967.

Van Doren, Carl. *Secret History of the American Revolution*. New York: Viking, 1941.

Walker, L.B. "Life of Margaret Shippen, Wife of Benedict Arnold." *Pennsylvania Magazine of History and Biography* (PMHB). Vol. XXIV-XXVI (1900-1902).

Wallace, Willard M. *Benedict Arnold, Traitorous Hero: The Life and Fortunes of Benedict Arnold*. New York: Harper & Brothers, 1954.

Wheeler, Richard. *Voices of 1776: The Story of the American Revolution in the Words of Those Who Were There*. New York: Meridian, 1991.

Wilson, Barry K. *Benedict Arnold: A Traitor in Our Midst*. Montreal: McGill-QueensUniversity Press, 2001.

## SOURCE NOTES

**Chapter One: Early Patterns**
1. Wallace, Willard M. *Benedict Arnold, Traitorous Hero*, p. 7.
2. Murphy, Jim. *The Real Benedict Arnold.* P. 19.
3. Wallace, p. 15.
4. Murphy, p. 37.
5. Murphy, p. 45-46.

**Chapter Two: Ticonderoga and Crown Point**
1. Martin, James Kirby. *Benedict Arnold, Revolutionary Hero; An American Warrior Reconsidered.* p. 68.
2. Wheeler, Richard. *Voices of 1776.* p. 26.
3. Wheeler, p. 23.
4. Martin, p. 82.
5. Martin, p. 100.

**Chapter Three: The Wilderness March**
1. Wheeler, p. 67.
2. Arnold, Benedict. *Diary/Memoirs.* p. 7.
3. Wallace, p. 65.
4. Washington to Arnold, Sept. 14, 1775, in Fitzpatrick, *Writings of George Washington*, vol. III, p. 491.
5. Van Doren, Carl. *Secret History of the American Revolution*, p. 207.
6. Scheer & Rankin, *Rebels and Redcoats: The American Revolution Through the Eyes of Those Who Fought It and Lived It*, p. 120.
7. Wheeler, p. 71.
8. Roberts, Kenneth, *March to Quebec: Journal of the members of the Arnold Expedition*, p. 337-338.
9. Arnold, p. 58-59.
10. Martin, p. 139.

11. Wheeler, p. 120.
12. Martin, p. 184.
13. Martin, p. 184.
14. Fitzpatrick, IV, p. 148.
15. Fitzpatrick, IV, p. 147.

**Chapter Four: Quebec: The Forlorn Hope**
1. Wallace, p. 79.
2. Wallace, p. 80.
3. Wheeler, p. 82.
4. Scheer & Rankin, p. 126; from a biography of Morgan, written in 1856.
5. Roberts, K., p. 537-538; Journal of Private George Morison.
6. Scheer & Rankin, p. 128.
7. Ketchum, Richard M. *Saratoga: Turning Point of America's Revolutionary War*, p. 35.
8. Wheeler, p. 115.
9. Wheeler, p. 115.
10. Ketchum, p. 36.
11. Ketchum, p. 36.
12. Martin, p. 203.
13. Martin, p. 244.
14. Martin, p. 184.
15. Martin, p. 233.
16. Murphy, p. 101.

**Chapter Five: Meantime . . .**
1. King, David C., *The United States and Its People*, p. 107.
2. Fitzpatrick, VI, p. 398-399.

**Chapter Six: America's First Naval Hero**
1. Martin, p. 248.
2. Van Doren, p. 111.
3. Both quotations in Wallace, p. 107.
4. Wallace, p. 111.

5. Martin, p. 249.
6. Murphy, p. 112.
7. Martin, p. 287.
8. Murphy, p. 113.
9. Martin, p. 288.
10. Murphy, p. 118.
11. Martin, p. 289.
12. Gould, Dudley C. *Benedict Arnold*, p. 16.

## Chapter 7: Heroics and Politics

1. Martin, p. 301.
2. Fitzpatrick, VII, p. 251-252.
3. Thacher, James. *Military Journal of the American Revolution*, p. 158.
4. Murphy, p. 121-122.
5. Murphy, p. 117.
6. Thacher, p. 159.
7. Arnold, p. 248.
8. Fitzpatrick, VII, p. 490.
9. Martin, p. 321.
10. Martin, p. 320-321.
11. Murphy, p. 128.
12. Martin, p. 322.
13. Murphy, p. 129.
14. Wallace, p. 125-126.
15. Murphy, p. 134-135.

## Chapter Eight: The Battle of Saratoga, Part I

1. Riedesel, Baroness Friederike von. *Letters and Journals Relating to the War of the American Revolution*, vol. I, p. 64.
2. Ketchum, p. 246.
3. Scheer & Rankin, p. 266.
4. Martin, p. 335.
5. Scheer & Rankin, p. 260.
6. Ketchum, p. 336.
7. Arnold, p. 284.
8. Ketchum, p. 344.
9. Ketchum, p. 344.

10. Scheer & Rankin, p. 276.
11. Scheer & Rankin, p. 276.
12. Wilkinson Memoirs, quoted in Scheer & Rankin, p. 279.
13. Wheeler, p. 222.
14. Wheeler, p. 222.
15. Martin, p. 383-384.
16. Ketchum, p. 366.
17. Martin, p. 382.
18. Ketchum, p. 368.
19. Riedesel, p. 214.
20. Murphy, p. 155.

## Chapter Nine: The Turning Point, Part II

1. Wheeler, p. 234.
2. Ketchum, p. 375.
3. Wheeler, p. 223.
4. Wheeler, p. 235.
5. Murphy, p. 156.
6. Ketchum, p. 394.
7. Wood, W.J., *Battles of the Revolutionary War, 1775-1784*. Chapel Hill, NC: Algonquin Books, 1990. Quoted in Murphy, p. 162.
8. Murphy, p. 161.
9. Scheer & Rankin, p. 281.
10. Murphy, p. 162.
11. Ketchum, p. 417.
12. Ketchum, p. 411.
13. Both quotes in Ketchum, p. 431.
14. Arnold, *Diary*, p. 256-257.
15. Murphy, p. 166.
16. Martin, p. 407.
17. Scheer & Rankin, p. 410.
18. Martin, p. 403.
19. Martin, p. 383-384.
20. Ketchum, 350-351.
21. Martin, p. 409.

## Chapter Ten: Twists and Turns

1. Martin, p. 416.

2. Martin, p. 416.
3. Van Doren, p. 172.
4. Martin, p. 425.
5. Wallace, p. 169.
6. Murphy, p. 176.
7. Murphy, p. 179.
8. Willard Sterne Randall, quoted in Murphy, p. 178.
9. John Richard Allen, quoted in Gould, p. 7.
10. Gould, p. 16.
11. Wallace, p. 172.
12. Walker, P.M.H.B., p. 35-36; 38.
13. Wallace, p. 174.
14. Van Doren, p. 192.
15. Dell, Pamela. *Benedict Arnold: From Patriot to Traitor*, p. 73.
16. Van Doren, p. 193.
17. Van Doren, p. 440.
18. Van Doren, p. 433.

**Chapter Eleven: The Tortured Road to Betrayal**
1. Wallace, p. 298.
2. Van Doren, p. 189.
3. Van Doren, p. 190.
4. Murphy, p. 196-197. Wallace, p. 186-187.
5. Wallace, p. 190.
6. Wallace, p. 191.
7. Gould, p. 64.
8. Wallace, p. 208.
9. Wallace, p. 216.
10. Murphy, p. 192.
11. Fitzpatrick, XVIII, p. 413.
12. Wallace, p. 215.
13. Gould, p. 50.
14. Gould, p. 57-58.
15. Van Doren, p. 194.
16. Wallace, p. 197.

**Chapter Twelve: "Treason of the Blackest Dye"**
1. Arnold, p. 263.
2. Wallace, p. 207.
3. Van Doren, p. 314.
4. Van Doren, p. 314.
5. Wallace, p. 228.
6. Andre, *Diary of John Andre*, p. 15.
7. Wheeler, p. 344-345.
8. Murphy, p. 212.
9. Wallace, p. 248.
10. Murphy, p. 212.
11. Murphy, p. 217.
12. Van Doren, p. 347.
13. Wheeler, p. 340.
14. Murphy, p. 218.
15. Murphy, p. 219.
16. Murphy, p. 219.
17. Andre's Journal, p. 108-109.
18. Andre's Journal, p. 110-111.
19. Wallace, p. 269.
20. Wallace, p. 269.
21. Wheeler, p. 352.
22. Arnold to Washington, Oct 4, 1780, in Sparks, *Writings of Washington*, VII, p. 541.
23. Wallace, p. 266.

**Chapter Thirteen: The Mystery of Peggy Shippen Arnold**
1. Ellet, Elizabeth, *Women of the American Revolution* (NY: Baker and Scribner, 1894, vol. 2, p. 216) quoted in Roberts, C. *Founding Mothers: The Women Who Raised Our Nation*, p. 129.
2. Wallace, p. 195.
3. Martin, p. 3.
4. Van Doren, p. 440.
5. Wallace, p. 196.
6. Wallace, p. 196.
7. Van Doren, p. 182-183.

8. Van Doren, p. 453.

9. Roberts, p. 129.

10. Van Doren, p. 198.

11. *Life of Colonel Pownell Phipps* (privately printed, 1894), in Taylor, S.G., p. 20.

12. Hart, A.B. *The Varick Court of Inquiry to Investigate the Implications of Colonel Richard Varick in the Arnold Treason*, quoted in Van Doren, p. 346.

13. Van Doren, p. 347; Varick testimony.

14. Van Doren, p. 347; Varick testimony.

15. Thacher, p. 471-472.

16. Scheer & Rankin, p. 384.

17. Scheer & Rankin, p. 384.

18. Wallace, p. 254.

19. Van Doren, p. 347.

20. Van Doren, p. 350.

21. Davis, M.L., *Memoirs of Aaron Burr*, vol. 1, p. 219.

22. Walker, P.M.H.B., p. 152-156, from Shippen Family Papers, *Burr Memoirs*.

23. Van Doren, p. 383.

24. Van Doren, p. 194.

25. Wallace, p. 261.

26. Van Doren, p. 387.

27. Wheeler, p. 351.

11. Taylor, p. 63-66.

**Epilogue**

1. Gould, p. 6.

**Chapter Fourteen:** *Nil Desperandum*: **The Final Years**

1. Thacher, p. 476.

2. Murphy, p. 225.

3. Wallace, p. 291.

4. P.M.H.B., XXV, p. 168; Wallace, p. 294.

5. P.M.H.B., XXV, p. 456-457.

6. P.M.H.B., XXV, p. 488-489.

7. Wallace, p. 292.

8. Duc de Brogle, *Memoirs of the Prince Talleyrand* (5 vols., NY, 1891). Quoted in Wallace, p. 300.

9. Gould, p. 6.

10. Taylor. *Some New Lights*, p. 59-60.

# INDEX

## A

Acland, John Dyke, 94

Acland, Lady, 94

Act of Reconciliation, 144

Adams, John, 42, 69

Admiralty Board, 128

Albany, New York

army hospital in, 93, 94, 98, 109

Burgoyne's push toward, 71, 73, 74, 84

defense of Lake Champlain and, 51

French push toward, 7

Schuyler's estate near, 20, 31

St. Leger's push toward, 76, 77

transporting of cannons to, 17

Allen, Ethan, 14–16, 18–20, 31, 44

Allen, John Richard, 111

American Legion, 144–45, 162, 164

American Revolution

Arnold's pivotal role in, 3, 71, 80, 176–77

Arnold's threat to success of, 163

signs of failure of, ix–x, 125, 126

Anburey, Thomas, 84, 87–88

Anderson, John. See Andre, John

Andre, John

Arnold's break-off of communication with, 116, 119

Arnold's letter to Washington about, 142, 160

bravery of, 139–40, 141

capture of, 134–36, 152

description of, 133, 140

early contact with Arnold, 115–17, 127, 147–48, 150

execution of, 138–41, 143, 159, 160

meeting with Arnold, 129, 132–34

picture of, 101

relationship with Peggy, 111, 150–51, 157, 176

Armstrong, John, 91

Arnold, Absalom King, 4

Arnold, Benedict (Benedict V's brother), 2, 4

Arnold, Benedict, I, 1

Arnold, Benedict, II, 1

Arnold, Benedict, III, 1–2

Arnold, Benedict, IV, 1–2, 4–5

Arnold, Benedict, V

character flaws of, 127–28, 163

children of

Benedict VI. See Arnold, Benedict, VI

Edward. See Arnold, Edward (Neddy)

George. See Arnold, George

Henry. See Arnold, Henry

John Sage, 168

with Peggy Shippen Arnold, 143, 160–61, 166–69. See also Arnold, Edward (Neddy)

Richard. See Arnold, Richard

convalescence of, 98–100, 109–10

damaged reputation of, 18–20, 53, 61

early life of, 1–11

childhood and family, 1–5

apprenticeship years, 5–7

young adulthood, 7–11

fearlessness of, 56

finances of, 123–24, 127

heroism of, 32, 44–45, 58–60, 62, 83–85, 176–77

humiliation of, 95–96, 98–100, 105, 120–23, 124–25

identities of

America's Hannibal, 32, 115

battlefield hero, 98, 99, 175

Captain Arnold, 8, 10, 13

Colonel Arnold, 13–19

criminal, 43–44, 45

Dark Angel, ix

Doctor Arnold, 7–8

evil genius, 59–60

horse jockey, 18, 58

misguided Patriot, ix–x

naval hero, 58–59, 62

traitor, ix, 100, 141–42, 161–63, 169, 175

Washington's fighting general, ix

last years of, 169–73

marriages of. See Arnold, Margaret (Peggy) Mansfield; Arnold, Margaret (Peggy) Shippen

Memoirs, 156–57

non-promotion of, 64–65

passion for Peggy, 176–77

# B

# C

Currency Act, 9

# D

Danbury, Connecticut, 66–67
Davis, M. L., 156–57
Dead River, 27–28, 102
Dearborn, Major, 90–92, 94, 98
Dearborn's light infantry, 81, 82, 90–92
De Blois, Elizabeth (Betsy), 63–64, 110, 112
Declaration of Independence, 48, 119, 143–44

Delaware River, 48, 61–62, 75
de Peyster, John Watts, 175
deserters, 126
Digby, William, 82
diphtheria, 2, 4
Downing, Samuel, 176
dysentery, 42

# E

East India Company, 10, 167
Easton, James, 18–20, 32, 43–44, 45, 52, 61
18th Irish regiment, 162
England
  Arnold's last years in, 169–73
  Arnold's new life in, 159, 166–67

See also British
Enos, Roger, 28–29
Enterprise (ship), 16–17
European Magazine, 173
Eustis, Dr., 152

# F

First Battle of Saratoga, 72, 80–85
food shortages in Philadelphia, 119–20
Forlorn Hope, 36
Fort Edward, 73, 74
Fortescue, John, 91
Fort Griswold, 165
Fort Schuyler. See Fort Stanwix
Fort Stanwix, 76–78, 79, 80
Fort Ticonderoga
  Arnold's attack on, 13–16, 17
  British outrage over attack at, 17–18, 19
  Carleton's planned attack on, 55
  Patriot defeat at, 73
  Patriot ships escape to, 57–58
  retreat to, 42, 43, 44
  ship outfitting at, 51–52
Fort Trumbull, 165

Fort William Henry, 7
"Fort Wilson," 119–20
France
  assistance to Washington, 164, 165, 166
  base at Rhode Island, 129, 163
  capture of Arnold in West Indies, 170, 176–77
  distrust of, ix–x, 126, 144, 161
  England's war with, 171
  entering of war, 95
  gifts from, 106
  Seven Years War and, 4–5, 6, 7
Franklin, Benjamin, 43, 52, 111, 127
Franks, David, 132, 136–38, 151–56
Fraser, Simon, 40, 41, 81, 90, 92
Freeman's Farm. See Battle of Saratoga
French and Indian War, 14
French-Canadians, 28, 30, 33–34

# G

Gage, Thomas, 10
Galloway, Grace, 109
Galloway, Joseph, 109
Ganesvoort, Peter, 76, 79
Gates, Horatio
  assistance to Washington, 61–62
  Battle of Camden and, 97–98
  betrayal/lack of support for Arnold, 66, 69, 70,
95–96, 98–99, 105

Brown's complaint to, 53
Congress and, 66, 79, 96–97, 105
defiance of Washington, 65–66, 70
at First Battle of Saratoga, 80–85
fleet-building with Arnold, 51–52
praise of Arnold, 58–59, 65
as replacement for Schuyler, 66, 70, 78–79
replacement with Greene, 97, 161–62
rise and fall of, 83, 96–98

# Y

# About the Author

David C. King is an award-winning author of more than seventy books for both adult and young-adult readers. He specializes in American history and biography, but has also written about other cultures, including Rwanda, Kenya, Bosnia, and Taiwan. He has written books in association with American Heritage and with the Smithsonian Institution, as well as shorter pieces for The World Bank, UNICEF, UNESCO, and Lincoln Center. His most recent book, *First People: An Illustrated History of American Indians* (NY: DK Publishing, 2008-2009) has won four national awards.

King and his wife Sharon live in the Berkshire Hills on the edge of New England. They have collaborated on several projects, including a biography of Charles Darwin and an award-winning history of the Statue of Liberty.